Savitz
Learning Resource Center
Glassboro State College
Glassboro, N. J. 08028

The Captive Princess

Other Books by Paul Morand

Novels
Flèche d'orient
France la doulce
L'Homme Pressé
Montociel
Hécate et ses chiens

Novelettes
Tendres stocks
  (Preface by Marcel Proust)
Ouvert la nuit
Fermé la nuit
Les Extravagants
  ("Milady" et "Monsieur Zéro")
La Folle amoureuse
Fin de siècle
Anthologie: I. Nouvelles du coeur
  II. Nouvelles des yeux

Essays
Journal d'un attaché d'ambassade
Monplaisir en littérature

Poems
Lampes à arc
Feuilles de température
Poèmes

Portraits
Paris-Tombouctou
Hiver Caraïbe
New York
Londres
Le Nouveau Londres

The
Captive Princess
Sophia Dorothea of Celle

by PAUL MORAND

Translated from the French by
Anne-Marie Geoghegan

AMERICAN HERITAGE PRESS
A Division of McGraw-Hill Book Company
New York   St. Louis   San Francisco   Toronto

DA
501
A2
M613

First published under the title *Ci-gît Sophie Dorothée de Celle*.
Copyright © Flammarion, 1968.

English translation copyright © 1972 by American Heritage Press,
a division of McGraw-Hill Book Company.
All rights reserved. Printed in the United States of America. No part
of this publication may be reproduced, stored in a retrieval system, or
transmitted, in any form or by any means, electronic, mechanical,
photocopying, recording, or otherwise, without the prior written
permission of the publisher.
123456789BPBP798765432

Library of Congress Cataloging in Publication Data
Morand, Paul, date
  The captive princess.
  Translation of Ci-gît Sophie Dorothée de Celle.
  1. Sophia Dorothea, consort of George I, King of
Great Britain, 1666-1726. I. Title.
DA501.A2M613   942.07'1'0924 [B]   75-39601
ISBN 0-07-043037-3

Contents

1. French Treasures in Germany   1
2. Iphigenia in Hanover   21
3. Sophia Dorothea, Hereditary Princess   29
4. The Rosenkavalier   47
5. Correspondence between Sophia Dorothea and
   Count von Königsmark   71
      Letters of Königsmark   79
      Letters of Sophia Dorothea   115
6. The Rosenkavalier Left No Traces   147
7. Aurora von Königsmark   161
8. The Secret Dungeons of Ahlden, 1694–1726   169
9. Monument to Sophia Dorothea   195
10. George Louis of Hanover, King of
    England (George I)   205

207374

11. The Stuart Rebellion   227
12. Sophia Dorothea's Son, The Prince of Wales,
    The Future George II of England   233
13. The Ghost of Sophia Dorothea Is Avenged   239
    History of the Correspondence and
    Bibliographical Note   253

The Captive Princess

1 / French Treasures in Germany

Madame d'Olbreuse, who became the Duchess of
Celle, wore all the graces of her native
land in Germany.

Voltaire, *The Century of Louis XIV*

September 1682

At six o'clock in the morning, Eléonore, Duchess of Celle,
lay in her state bed, her hair already in order. The
canopy of the four-poster was supported by gilded cherubs
from whose chubby fists floated masses of crimson silk
that was embellished with Portuguese embroidery shot
with gold thread. This was the rich frame for the Duchess's slightly faded beauty. Under English lace, her black
curls glinting with white recalled the two ebony cabinets
inlaid with pewter that flanked the bed.

The Duchess, whose maiden name was d'Olbreuse,
had in her hand a tortoiseshell fan with which she was
ready to ward off the first attack of the sun, already beginning to climb the counterpane. The smoothness of
her striking complexion was marred only by smallpox
scars. Her pink negligee revealed an ample bosom which
rose and fell as she sighed contentedly.

The Duchess of Celle was soon to marry off her daughter, Sophia Dorothea, the richest heiress of the Holy Roman Empire, to August Frederick, the son of Duke Anthony Ulrich of Brunswick-Wolfenbüttel, a neighbor. Her
wishes fulfilled, the Duchess resembled a caryatid re-
lieved of the weight of its entablature.

This bedroom, decorated like a salon, this ducal bed to which her ladies in waiting bowed as they went by even when it was empty (as was the custom at Versailles), the small round tables loaded with objets d'art, the marquetry wardrobes, the Boulle table clocks—all of these things had successfully banished the heavy German furniture. A foreign influence had taken over Celle, banished the cumbersome Medieval antiques, and transformed this duchy, up to now ruled by the tastes of its neighbors, Hanover and Holland. German castles look like military hospitals or barracks, and from the outside the Castle of Celle, with its penitentiary walls, remained a citadel crowned by storks' nests.

With gentle insistence the Duchess gradually and single-handedly transformed the interior of the castle into a boudoir. Slowly but surely this native of France, lost in a remote northern land, asserted her reign. The hostility of these places and the people recalled to Eléonore her native Poitou. There her Huguenot family had lived in hiding since Henry III's time, in the midst "of a Babylon drunk with the blood of the faithful," constantly threatened with seeing themselves on the bishop's black list, for the first persecutions of the Protestants had taken place in Poitou. She had been hidden in cellars, in woodcutters' huts in the forest, lest she be dragged off by Catholics who would attempt to convert her. In the woods she had heard the priests crying: "Kill, kill!" She had watched the flames fanned at the stake by the sermons of the Jesuit Father Bourdaloue, and she had seen the mass denials of the faith that followed.

The Marquis d'Olbreuse and his daughters had come to Holland by sea. There Eléonore was one of the great flock of fugitives, living on public charity and by

gathering edible snails. In this pleasant atmosphere
of liberty it was possible to survive. Links among the
exiles remained close despite the scrutiny of the Count
d' Avaux, who represented Louis XIV at The Hague, and
despite the constant fear of a French invasion aimed at
suppressing the Protestant heresy. (During the reign of
Jan De Witt, from 1653 to 1672, the French had almost
taken over Holland.) Among the French officers who had
enlisted in the army of the Prince of Orange was the
Prince of Tarente, a member of the house of La Trémoille.
He headed several French regiments called the Glory of
the Refugees, which distinguished themselves in Holland, as did other members of the La Trémoille family
in the armies of Hesse, and as did the French Huguenot
musketeers in the service of the Elector of Brandenburg—
who fought for the King of Prussia.[1]

Alexandre Desmier, Marquis d'Olbreuse, and his two
beautiful daughters, jostled in the throng of seventy
thousand French refugees, finally found asylum in Breda.
The Princess of Tarente had also settled there and, having
known the d'Olbreuse family in Poitou, she took them
under her wing. She had the reputation of being extremely frivolous and her salon was the most popular and
gayest in Breda, then the most animated town in Holland.
Charles II had lived in exile there; the diplomats of the
Congress of 1667 had danced and signed a peace treaty
there. Masquerades, balls, and French entertainments
were constantly in progress inside these small houses
with their tarred brick façades. At one of these parties
Eléonore made a great hit disguised as a nymph. This
France in exile was a miniature Versailles—that Ver-

---

[1] ". . . Protestants taking with them out of France their skills and their hatred of
the King of France, urged on by the revocation of the Edict of Nantes and by the
religious persecution." Voltaire, *Century of Louis XIV*.

sailles that everyone detested, even though to be accepted in Breda one had to have ridden in the royal coaches at that same Versailles. Everything French was in vogue; even the Dutch imitated the French, dressing their retainers in the French style, smoking in the Protestant churches, replacing their steel door knockers with silver ones, and burying their relatives by lantern light. French words infiltrated German and Dutch: *sottisen, lacheteten, fadaisen,*[2] a confidence trick was a *foppa*.[3] Profiting by cheap French labor, the Dutch built houses "as the dauphin [of France] did."

In her bed the Duchess recalled those bitter years in Breda which had gradually mellowed in her memory with the passage of time; Breda, where her French countrymen, with typically Latin nonchalance, walked the streets in slippers, called to one another from their boxes at the theater, learned to enjoy java coffee sweetened with honey in the cafés. They made fun of the spotless Dutch streets and traveled the frozen canals in sledges representing gilded swans. In short, they took on the manners of the royal court at Versailles, where Eléonore and her sister Angélique had been presented before the revocation of the Edict of Nantes. The Duchess saw herself again in nearby Holland, lost in the extraordinary throng of French noblemen and preachers, Jewish diamond merchants who had fled from Antwerp to Amsterdam, peasants from the Cévennes and bankers from Nîmes, Huguenot doctors who in France were refused the cadavers they needed for research, makers of thermometers, microscopes, or clocks from Paris. This was

---

[2] In French, *sottise*, foolishness; *lâcheté*, cowardice; *fadaise*, nonsense. — Trans.
[3] *Foppa*, from the French *faux-pas*. — Trans.

a world in which the psalms mingled with gavottes, where Louis XIV was detested, but where everyone tried to learn the latest news from his court by perusing the gazettes each morning in the chocolate houses at tables crowded with clay pipes, charcoal braziers, and spittoons.

This was Breda in 1655 where Eléonore's life began to take shape. Every day her protectress, the Princess of Tarente, would entertain not only distinguished refugees but all passing travelers of some distinction in Europe and the Holy Roman Empire. At her house they would dance, play cards, stage plays. Because she had been born Princess of Hesse-Kassel and was the aunt of the celebrated Sophia of Hanover, she received the Hanoverian princes as relatives.

In particular she received George Wilhelm of Brunswick-Lüneburg, whom Eléonore was destined to marry.

After years of wandering, the bulk of them spent in Venice, George Wilhelm appeared in Breda, so close to his home and yet in its customs a sort of northern Venice. The Princess of Tarente opened her salon to him, and there the great attraction was Eléonore d'Olbreuse. They acted in plays together; from that they passed to French lessons; then from grammar to declarations of love. George Wilhelm offered his fortune to the young French woman, but she would not surrender. "This girl who belongs to the Princess of Tarente" (the Princess Palatine wrote, as one would have said of a servant) was a woman of honor and even in exile showed her noble origins. She knew how to be cruel, like the heroine of a novel by Mlle. de Scudéry. George Wilhelm became more and more infatuated and would willingly have consented to marry her, but by signing a contract with his family he had relinquished the right ever to marry. He could only offer Eléonore a morganatic marriage,[4] a sort of halfway union valid before God and man, but void as far as children of the marriage were concerned.

At this moment Christian Louis, the Duke of Celle, died suddenly. George Wilhelm had to leave Breda and rush home to seize the duchy from his younger brother, Jean Frederick, who was about to take it for himself.

While he was away Eléonore thought over his proposal. She was virtuous, but also wise. The Princess of Tarente assured her that she would never find a better match; that this union would enable the Marquis, her father, to live out his old age in peace; that in any case she could hardly remain an old maid in Breda all her life without the least hope of ever returning to France. Moreover, her memories of Niort, Parthenay, the gentle countryside of the parish of Usseaux, and the whole of Saintonge, were gradually fading.

In melancholy moments, Eléonore could still visualize her native Marais,[5] but more and more vaguely—the canals shaded by overhanging trees shot through with sunlight; the coves, almost a foretaste of Holland, in which boats glided past at ground level loaded with hay or cattle, steered by the woman with her oar, propelled with a long pole by the man; the old gardener who sometimes took Eléonore fishing for eels under a swarm of dragonflies.

In Hanover, George Wilhelm assumed the title of Duke of Celle, and still Eléonore hesitated. She was twenty-six, the age at which marriageable girls become apprehensive.

---

[4] From German law: *Maurgjan*, to restrain (Littre, *Dictionnaire de la Langue Francaise*)

[5] Marais is the name of a district of France in the old province of Vendée. The word means marshland. — Trans.

Two very amiable letters arrived from Princess Sophia, George Wilhelm's sister-in-law, offering Eléonore a place as a lady in waiting at the Osnabrück court. It was an adequate pretext for not breaking off her relationship with George Wilhelm, and the promise of a warm welcome won her over. She crossed the frontier and was met on the German side.

Ernst August, the Prince Bishop of Osnabrück, and his haughty wife, Princess Sophia, had been most enthusiastic about the projected morganatic marriage. It seemed to guarantee their own future, for the children of such marriages could not succeed to a crown.

To appreciate the Prince Bishop's satisfaction calls for some knowledge of the constitutional rules of the house of Brunswick-Lüneburg, which descended directly from the powerful Guelphs of the Middle Ages and which now ruled Hanover.[6] When the last duke had died, he divided his domain among his seven sons. These sons had quickly realized that, at this rate of partition, the Hanover of which they were so proud would soon be no more than a clutch of small states without influence in the vast Holy Roman Empire. Thus they concluded a family pact stipulating that only the eldest could marry and have children, while the others would remain celibate.

Ceaseless wars fortunately absorbed the surplus of these prolific families, and toward the middle of the seventeenth century only three of the seven states remained: the duchy of Hanover, the duchy of Celle, and the prince-bishopric of Osnabrück. Of the brothers, four remained. The eldest, the Duke of Hanover, having

---

[6] The Guelphs of Brunswick were the fourth oldest princely house of the Empire, older than the Hapsburgs. They were the sixteenth in line (out of forty-three) in the Council of Princes of the Holy Roman Empire. — Trans.

already chosen celibacy, George Wilhelm, Duke of Celle and second in line, ought to have been designated to perpetuate the reigning branch of the Brunswicks. A fiancee was found for him. She was an excellent match, not because she was rich (for the Palatine princes were a needy lot), but because of her bloodline. She was Princess Sophia, daughter of the Palatine King of Bohemia and granddaughter on her mother's side of the English King James I. In addition she was majestic, learned, and austere. These virtues terrified the Duke of Celle, who was already too inclined to flee marriage in favor of a sybaritic existence. He thus decided to abdicate his right to the Hanoverian succession in favor of his next younger brother, Ernst August, of whom he was particularly fond. In so doing, he almost came to blows with his youngest brother, who claimed the succession for himself.

However, the Duke of Celle prevailed and irrevocably gave up his rights to this younger brother, Ernst August, Prince Bishop of Osnabrück. In addition, he agreed never to marry, although the value of such family promises is well known. The agreement simply gave George Wilhelm a bad conscience, a sort of guilt complex, which was the key to his behavior when he did marry. Princess Sophia had not only been ignored during these proceedings, but actually passed on to Ernst August in the bargain. It is probable that the proud Sophia, who would have preferred George Wilhelm, resigned herself to Ernst August only for lack of a better prospect. She never pardoned the Duke of Celle for having spurned her so cavalierly and she forgave his French wife even less for having been preferred to her.

At the Osnabrück castle the Prince Bishop and Princess

Sophia received Eléonore in the most friendly way imaginable; they embraced her, and, preceded by the inevitable fanfare, mounted the grand staircase, and showed her to her apartment. Eléonore was both touched and pleased by this welcome. She was being treated with honor. She accepted the morganatic marriage, which was celebrated in September 1665. The Prince Bishop and Princess Sophia placed their signatures under those of the bride and groom and Eléonore was granted the title of Countess of Harburg, one of her husband's domains.

But things only appeared to be going well. From the start Eléonore's new position was imperceptibly undermined and she was gradually deprived of the rank to which she appeared to have been elevated. She came down to meals with the ducal family preceded by trumpets, but she was seated at a small table off by herself and she did not eat. Later, in her room, she was given the leftovers from the banquet—huge sausages resting on mountains of red cabbage, which she loathed. With the help of her sister, Angélique, whom she had brought to Osnabrück and who had made an excellent match by marrying the Count of Reuss, Eléonore cooked light, French dishes in her apartments. This habit was soon discovered by the Hanoverian princes, who treated it as a huge joke. Princess Sophia, so friendly in the beginning and so apparently satisfied with her morganatic sister-in-law who was discreet and "knew how to keep her place," became haughty. Eléonore quickly understood that at the Castle of Osnabrück she had just about the status of a governess. Her pride was deeply wounded, and she profited from her growing influence on her husband, who was very much in love with her, to ask for and achieve their departure from Osnabrück for the

Castle of Celle, where they settled permanently. There, as mistress in her own house, she would be able to banish the memory of the humiliations she had endured.

And it was at Celle, a year after her wedding, that Sophia Dorothea, her beloved daughter, was born.

At Celle too began the implacable feud between the two sisters-in-law; between the haughty, pure-blooded German, Sophia, and the newly arrived French interloper. Every day Eléonore understood more clearly the distance that Sophia felt separated them; a gap infinitely broader than that between her father, the Marquis d'Olbreuse and the least of his French peasants. For the royal or princely houses of the Holy Roman Empire, dating at least from the time of Charlemagne, as did these Guelphs, a Marquis from Poitou was "without birth and without family." Eléonore could also see how little meaning her morganatic marriage had for the Hanoverians. Now that she had been initiated into the complexities of German common law, she better understood this family pact, which had seemed so absurd and even ridiculous to her before.

Northern Germany at the time still resembled the feudal land of the year 1000.[7] These Germans were as proud of the purity of their blood as were the Spaniards; they were fascinated by Italy and yet despised it; they hated, yet imitated the French; they were faithful subjects of the Empire, but separated by religion from the Emperor. They fought everywhere magnificently, yet shrewdly sold themselves to the highest bidder. Simple, brutal, physically courageous and morally weak, they

---

[7] In the *History of the House of Brunswick* (Hanover) may be found a genealogy of the Guelphs family and their exploits until the year 700.

seemed to Eléonore implausible, hero-comic figures. But she had to understand them in order to use them in the endless struggle against Osnabrück and in order to consolidate her uneasy position.

With the weapons of a woman who is loved, weapons at once weak and yet so powerful, Eléonore had exerted constant pressure on the Duke. To begin with, she had induced him to have the Emperor make her a Countess of the Empire *(Reichsgräfin)* because in its war against the Turks Vienna needed the help of the duchy of Celle, or at least of its mercenaries.

Osnabrück still had advantages: Sophia Dorothea could never succeed to Celle, for the dukedom would revert to George Louis, Princess Sophia's son.

Eléonore then played her trump card: In 1676 she managed to have her daughter legitimized, thus annulling the effect of the morganatic marriage and of the family pact, while at the same time making Sophia Dorothea the richest heiress in Germany. Two years later the tenacious Eléonore confirmed her victory: Vienna agreed to transform her morganatic union into a legitimate marriage. She became the Duchess of Lüneburg-Celle and, as Pollnitz says, "there was nothing greater she could have desired." The house of Osnabrück had been routed.

But their revenge followed their defeat: the Duke of Hanover died and his brother, the Prince Bishop, succeeded. Keeping Osnabrück, Ernst Augustus and Princess Sophia also became Duke and Duchess of Hanover, and were henceforth equal to Celle. The seventeenth and eighteenth centuries were the heydays of espionage. Indeed, at any court the curiosity would have been the man who was not a spy. One had to spy to defend one's position, one's family, one's country, or to become rich. Everyone was in someone's pay. The 600-odd states of the Holy Roman Empire all eavesdropped on one another, and the more important ones had secret agents in the great foreign courts at Vienna, Paris, London, The Hague, even Turin or Madrid. These agents duplicated or nullified the efforts of the official representatives of the German states.

Ernst August had a powerful spy at the court of his dear brother, George Wilhelm. This was Count von Bernstorff, Prime Minister of the Duchy of Celle, an extremely intelligent, deceitful, selfish, and clever man who came to have more and more influence over his master. For more than forty years he played a diabolical double role, always with success. The Duke of Celle was naive, jovial, without ambition, happy with his wife and beloved daughter, proud of his hunts and of the 370 English horses in his stables. He was proud also of Eléonore's beauty and grace, and of the little Sophia Dorothea, for whom he intended to arrange a worthy marriage. He had almost arranged a union with the second son of the King of Denmark, but the project fell through, doubtless owing to some maneuver by Princess Sophia: She had said angrily: "A King's son for that little bastard!"

This remark had been reported to the Duchess of Celle. Six years previously the Duchess had affianced the "little bastard" to a pure-blooded Brunswick, he too a descendant of Henry the Lion. Unfortunately the fiance's head had been blown off at the siege of Philippsburg—a misfortune welcomed by Princess Sophia. However, this only postponed the matchmaking. Now Duke Anthony Ulrich of Wolfenbüttel was about to arrive with his second son to ask for and obtain Sophia Dorothea's hand.

This marriage would make the girl the equal of the greatest ladies in Germany.[8]

The Wolfenbüttels were old and loyal friends of Eléonore's. A further advantage, in her view, was that the family was on the point of converting to Catholicism and thus was looked on most favorably by Louis XIV. Through them Eléonore hoped to regain title to her confiscated lands in Poitou. In addition, the dukes of Brunswick-Wolfenbüttel were entirely taken by French influence and, despite the persecutions of the Huguenots, Eléonore had remained profoundly French. This was a real stroke of luck for all the Calvinist refugees who gathered around her in Celle and who could be sure of a post in the army or at her court. The Duchy of Celle had gradually become a sort of French beachhead between Holland and Brandenburg. Eléonore had really made it her own, this little capital of ten thousand souls lost among the sands of the Aller River. She had transformed the moats into French gardens; her table was always open to refugees, and the renowned cuisine was free of venison and red cabbage. She built a court theater where the Duke had such fun running from box to box and from the foyer to the corridors that he did not even watch the show. Handsomely paid dancers came from Paris at each carnival season, and the latest novelties arrived daily from Versailles: repeater clocks or barometers in cases fashioned by Boulle. The *poupée*[9] from the Rue Saint-Honoré, which every spring brought the latest Paris fashions to the courts of the north, now stopped in Celle,

---

[8] According to the custom of the Empire, the title of Princess was given only to those who were princesses by birth, except in the case of a special dispensation by the Emperor. (Pollnitz, *Secret History of the Duchess of Hanover*, London, 1707.)

[9] Translator's note: The *poupée* was a doll which served as a traveling model for the designers.

with its wigs, purses, shoes, and lace ruffles. At the castle, the old military regime was changed. Gone were the meals announced by a flourish of trumpets at eleven in the morning and four in the afternoon. Now a page reminded the diners that it was forbidden to exchange insults at table, to throw bones or bread at each other, to dip into a dish with their hands (hitherto only the Duke had had the right to use a large fork) and to pocket choice tidbits.[10] It was no longer necessary to cart off the drunks in a wheelbarrow at the end of the meal. The French, especially those from Aunis and Saintonge,[11] were better paid than employees recruited locally. Among the huntsmen, for example, a French whipper-in of hounds earned 421 thalers a year while his German counterpart received 228.

It had taken Eléonore seventeen years to achieve these results, but from then on Celle was her affair, her pride and joy, her entertainment, her impregnable domain, the reward for so many years of married love, and also of so many sacrifices and humiliations. Her court was so French that a passing Frenchman, invited to the Duke's table, exclaimed naively: "How delightful, my lord. There is no foreigner here except you!"

But this gallicization, which was perhaps excessive, worked against Eléonore. It was little by little exploited by Bernstorff and subtly opposed by the Duke, who became less and less subject to his wife's influence.

To ensure her own and her daughter's future, Eléonore had persuaded her husband to make her some large presents. In a few years, five important domains had become hers, to the fury of Duke Ernst August, who saw

---

[10] Ed. Vehse, *Geschichte des Hofe Braunschweig* (Hamburg, 1853).
[11] Near Poitou, Eléonore's home province. — Trans.

the piecemeal division of the estate that he considered his—until the day, that is, when Sophia Dorothea was legitimized and so became the sole and incontestable heir. To placate his favorite brother, the Duke of Celle often gave him money. Not that Ernst August was greedy for money, but he loved his pleasures and, being ostentatious and fond of ceremony, he was constantly short of cash. When the Duke of Celle gave his wife the lovely domain of Wilhemsburg on the Elbe River, opposite Hamburg, he appeased Ernst August by giving him 18,000 thalers. Celle could afford these expensive transactions, for the Duchy was well governed, and expanded and grew richer every day. By contrast, Osnabrück was needy and Hanover was constantly deep in debt, owing to the lavish spending of its duke.

There was a knock on the door and Sophia Dorothea entered her mother's room. She was sixteen and her beauty lit up the room, making the hythological scenes painted on the ceiling and the pink clouds bearing goddesses that adorned the walls appear to pale.

Sophia Dorothea's features and figure were perfect. She recalled the beauty of Mlle. d'Olbreuse in earlier days, but without her firmness and resolution. The difference in age distinguished the two women less than the signs of age and weariness around her mother's eyes. In contrast to her mother, Sophia Dorothea's little forehead pressed forward as if she were ready to make a triumphant pounce. Her graceful, supple gestures, her hair gleaming like mahogany, her shining dark brown eyes, revealed the delight to be alive of a young animal.

Eléonore looked at her daughter adoringly. Sophia was her creation, her success, her triumph. From the socially worthless child of a morganatic marriage, she had made the most sought after princess in the Holy Roman Empire.

Sophia Dorothea was not only Eléonore's pride and joy, but also her pleasure, her entertainment, her beautiful doll to dress, to coif, to adorn so as to be driven around the country in a little coach drawn by ponies and made to wave sweetly to subjects who adored their ravishing princess. Indeed, until the end, the people of Celle adored her and wept for her as though she were their own child.

With this upbringing Sophia Dorothea could have become monstrously vain and selfish. Instead she was goodhearted, generous, and straightforward. Consequently, her only weakness—a most dangerous one—was a profound need to be loved.

"My dear angel," the Duchess said, "I was longing to see you. Your father is still asleep, and you must have your chocolate with me at this little table. I want you close by. I never see enough of you."

"And yet you want to marry me off," said the girl, smiling. "You'll see me a lot less then, won't you?"

"No, of course not. Wolfenbüttel is a friendly court, and it's not far from here. I will see you as often as I want to, and even if I couldn't, I would make the sacrifice so that my little daughter could become a Most Serene Highness. You deserve it. You are so beautiful."[12]

In the dark courtyard of the castle, its ocher-colored walls barely distinguishable in the half-light of dawn,

---

[12] "She is extremely well built," wrote the *Mercure Galant* the day after Sophia Dorothea arrived in Hanover. "She has medium blond hair, a little dimple in her chin, a beautiful and finely textured complexion, a lovely neck. She dances, plays the clavichord, and sings perfectly. Very witty and vivacious, she has a rich and inspired imagination as a result of her wide reading. She was born with very good taste, which has been enhanced by the care that was taken with her education. . . . She speaks well on every subject and enters shrewdly into everything that people tell her."

a traveling coach had just arrived. When she heard the clatter of the wheels and the horseshoes, Eléonore said: "It can't be the Wolfenbüttels; it's too early. Perhaps it is their advance party? If so, they will be here soon, so go and dress, my dearest. I will ring for my maids."

In Hanover, Ernst August was having a nap after lunch when his frightened major-domo abruptly woke him. A messenger had just arrived from Celle at full gallop with an urgent message from Count von Bernstorff. When he read it, the Duke almost collapsed with shock. Bernstorff wrote that he had only by chance heard of the arrival the very next morning of Duke Anthony Ulrich of Wolfenbüttel and his son for the official engagement of the young man and Sophia Dorothea. "Wolfenbüttel, Wolfenbüttel," repeated the Duke, panicking Wolfenbüttel, his hated cousin, the Catholic, the friend of the French! This meant that when George Wilhelm died, Hanover would be unified no longer to the benefit of George Louis, but under a Wolfenbüttel. Sophia Dorothea's enormous dowry was slipping from Ernst August's hands to enrich the enemy. It was easy to grasp the danger of this move that had been so cleverly and secretly arranged by Eléonore. But what could he do to oppose her? Who could he send to Celle to influence his indecisive brother, George Wilhelm? Ernst August's exaggerated demands had lost him all his credit, and his ministers no longer counted. But why not his wife? Only Sophia, with her stature and prestige, could convince her brother-in-law. But first he had to persuade her to do it. It is easy to imagine how this proud lady resisted the prospect of humbling herself before "the little clot of dirt," her sister-in-law. . . . In Princess

Sophia reason dominated feeling. She realized what was at stake and ordered her traveling coach to be made ready.[13]

Hanover is just over thirty miles from Celle, but the roads of the time were terrible, and during the present season almost impassable. Rudely jostled, Princess Sophia traveled all night to reach Celle in the early morning. The honor guard, bewildered to see the princely colors of Hanover, allowed the coach to pass.

Princess Sophia brushed past the bodyguard and, followed at a distance by the breathless page on duty, hurried up the grand staircase. She strode quickly through the reception rooms, then through the antechambers of the private apartments, and burst into her brother-in-law's bedroom. The Duke of Celle, wearing a batik dressing gown, was seated at his dressing table. Since his marriage to Mlle. d'Olbreuse the haughty Sophia had not darkened the doors of Celle, and the Duke was so astounded to see her that he was unable to utter a word. On the table in front of him were his short, morning wig, his snuffboxes, his mirror, and his morning cup of bouillon. His shirt, already warmed, lay on a stool, and his jacket was ready near the white faïence stove.

Princess Sophia imperiously seized a chair, sat down close to George Wilhelm, and spoke to him in a voice that was almost low, for she had seen that the door to Eléonore's room was ajar. Affecting both familiarity and gaiety, she spoke in low German, a dialect of which Eléonore knew not a word.

Still in her bed, the Duchess of Celle overheard the

---

[13] *Histoire secrète . . .* (Anon.), 1707.

conversation and shouted questions. But her husband only begged her to be silent.

George Wilhelm was completely taken in by Sophia's eloquent and never-ending talk. With a remarkable psychological sense, she flattered all his instincts, his feelings, ambitions, and most secret wishes. She complained that they never saw him and deplored the gap between two brothers who had been so close to each other since their earliest years, when they had traveled the world together. She conjured up the possibility of a ninth electorate that would benefit him. (It was later created, but it benefited Ernst August instead.) Finally she spoke in glowing terms of her eldest son, George Louis, of his great merit and his brilliant future. After all, did he not have some chance of becoming the King of England after the death of Queen Anne, who had designated him as her successor? In any case, could he not have aspired to the hand of any European princess? But, no, he wanted only Sophia Dorothea because his dearest wish, and that of his parents, was to see Hanover reunified under a single crown.

Touched, dazzled, and finally convinced, George Wilhelm consented to everything Sophia wanted. Now he had only to inform his wife that he had granted their daughter's hand to his nephew, George Louis.

The Duke of Celle was an impressive man, heavily built, with big blue eyes and red hair that grew bushily practically down to his eyebrows. Although he tried to remain calm as he entered his wife's room, he had the quick temper of the weak-willed. His fleshy features reddened as his blood quickened. He was without his wig and flecks of shaving cream behind his ears showed that he had been surprised at his toilet. "I don't know what this is all about," the Duchess thought, "but George Wilhelm has just had a discussion in which he was the loser."

As he advanced, the Duke betrayed increasing embarrassment. His troubled conscience showed in the shaking of his large hands.

"I have just had a long and most important talk with our sister-in-law, Sophia," he began.

"Sophia here, at seven in the morning?"

"She has come from Hanover after traveling all night."

"Why didn't you let me know right away?"

"She thought . . . Sophia and I thought, that we ought to have a private conversation since the future of the whole house of Brunswick-Lüneburg is at stake. Madame, I have just granted the hand of our daughter, Sophia Dorothea, to my nephew, George Louis. Be so kind as to dress so that you can receive Sophia . . . and make yourself ready for the arrival of the Wolfenbüttels,"[14] he added with a grimace at the thought of the unpleasant moments that would follow their coming.

---

[14] It may be of some interest to read the *Notes sur le duche de Brunswick* by Stendhal and of his journey to Wolfenbüttel on July 6, 1807. He describes his hatred for sauerkraut ("beastly food"), the icy eiderdowns, the tasteless fruit, and all that Mlle. d'Olbreuse suffered a century earlier.

2 / Iphigenia in Hanover

These tense moments at Celle have been recounted in such detail by Wilkins that it almost seems as if he himself had been present.[1] It is possible that he found his description in the book written by the Duke of Wolfenbüttel, who in turn probably had it from Mlle. de Knesebeck, who was a witness because she lived at the Castle at the time of the betrothal and whose integrity made her a reliable observer.

When the Duke broke the news, Eléonore felt the ground crumbling under her. She saw herself the laughingstock of her own domain, her worst enemies in power, her only daughter sacrificed to a stranger, probably a debauched brüte. This powerful and beautiful woman fell on her knees before her husband, entreating, imploring, sobbing.

George Wilhelm shrugged his shoulders. He found the whole thing more ridiculous than moving, and, so far as his wife was concerned, he was right. What objection could she make to such an excellent match? Her daughter would be marrying a prince renowned for his merit; one day she would reign not over the tiny state of Wolfenbüttel but over the vast state of Hanover-

---

[1] W. H. Wilkins, *The Love of an Uncrowned Queen* (1900).

Osnabrück-Celle, and she might even succeed to one of the greatest thrones of Europe.

In fact, Eléonore's grief showed that she was rather narrow-minded. In her place a woman like Madame de Maintenon, Louis XIV's mistress and later his second wife, would instantly have seen the advantages of this match. In this instance, it was not Eléonore but Princess Sophia who had been humiliated, for she, after all, was forced to come and solicit the hand of the daughter of "Madame" d'Olbreuse of whom the Princess Palatine said: "No one decent would have agreed to serve the Princess of Tarente, but since the d'Olbreuse woman is a nobody, that is of no importance . . . that intriguer, offspring of a French family, thus of an imposture. . . ." For these grand German ladies the French nobility hardly counted, for it was incapable of making up a family tree after the year 1000 without including a misalliance. Leibnitz in his *History of the House of Brunswick-Hanover* describes these Guelphs as proving their worth until the time of Charlemagne. Their great centuries were the tenth and eleventh; decadence set in from the thirteenth century. But now, through the miraculous effect of this marriage, the "person," the "little clot of dirt," would be one of theirs! It would end their contempt, their cruel words, their insults! Henceforth no one at the court of Hanover would dare attack the mother of the princess who was the hereditary Princess. Eléonore, obsessed by the vanished dream of a pleasant marriage for her daughter, had not even thought of the revenge which she was destined to enjoy on the day of Ernst August's death. Then Princess Sophia would become simply the dowager duchess while Sophia Dorothea would be the reigning Duchess.

Sophia Dorothea was even more upset than her mother at the prospect of changing fiancés. She shouted, sobbed, stormed, smashed to smithereens the portrait of George Louis, set in diamonds, that her future mother-in-law had brought for her. She insisted: "I will not marry the pig snout" (George Louis' nickname in Hanover). Her desperation and despair can only be explained by the assumption that Eléonore, confiding her bitterness to her daughter, had described the court of Hanover as a den of wild beasts and pitiless enemies.

After all, it has taken two world wars and several revolutions to wean princesses of the blood away from the deep-rooted conviction that to be queen is the ideal vocation.

When Sophia Dorothea was face to face with Princess Sophia, her father ordered her to kiss her aunt's hand. Instead the girl lost her color and fainted in her mother's arms.

These two women, their lively brown eyes wet with tears, contrasted sharply to the rigid blue-eyed Germans —Princess Sophia's dark blue, George Wilhelm's a watery light blue.

"Come and greet your aunt," said the Duke impassively to Sophia Dorothea.

Princess Sophia watched these tears and her niece's collapse without saying a word, as though they were completely inappropriate manifestations of emotion. Everything about her indicated that she found this bourgeois quarrel insupportable—her stony face of a judge on the bench, her artificial complexion under ash-colored hair, her heavy chin sunk into her haughty neck, her look of total indifference. As if deaf to the sobs and entreaties, she condescended to become the kind lady, opening her arms to her niece with a false kindness intended to make everyone feel the superiority of court manners over the ill-placed whims of a tearful little girl.

The twelve-foot-thick vault trembled as another coach rattled noisily over the rounded pebbles of the courtyard.

Armed Wolfenbüttel footmen in ceremonial livery sprang to the ground. All that remained for the Duke was to come down and greet his neighbors.

The three women confronted each other in silence. Princess Sophia was completely in control of herself as she watched Eléonore weep for her lost paradise. Sophia Dorothea was as white as a statue in the park outside, the very image of innocence sacrificed for reasons of state. The Princess, cool and frighteningly collected, considered her achievement and was disgusted by the exaggeration inevitable in all suffering. She showed neither embarrassment nor emotion. She was clearly a friend of Leibnitz, the philosopher, who habitually thought in universal terms, for whom the particular was of no interest. She seemed to look at human passions through a telescope.

Tense as a drawn bow, Sophia Dorothea cried to her mother: "I will never leave you. I would rather die at Celle."

Princess Sophia shrugged her shoulders at this frivolous announcement. She considered love a thoroughly vulgar feeling. This girl, whose mother was born a nobody, ought to be only too happy to be accepted by her son and to become heiress to the Duchy of Hanover.

The Duke rushed into the room again, most upset. He had just informed the Wolfenbüttels of the decision. With a curious lack of tact, he had even invited them to the engagement party. Deeply offended, the Wolfenbüttels had left immediately. This news made Eléonore even angrier and caused Sophia Dorothea to burst into tears again. George Wilhelm resumed his majestic composure, sickened by this domestic tragedy as a professional soldier might be by a civil war.

That the Duke of Celle was deaf to the entreaties of his beloved daughter, and that in the twinkling of an eye he should have changed from the Wolfenbüttel to the Osnabrück camp would be astonishing if the fuse on the bomb had not been lit long before. The proud and happy Eléonore had unwittingly walked into an ambush. Bernstorff, in the pay of Ernst August, was probably also working for William III, the Stadholder of Holland. William was married to Mary of England; he was not anxious to see George Louis seek the hand of the other English princess, Anne. Indeed, he had secretly encouraged the union of the two Hanoverian cousins. Bernstorff had accordingly prepared the Duke of Celle; the eloquence and vivacity of Princess Sophia did the rest.

The next day, Ernst August and his son arrived in Celle. A courier sent by Princess Sophia had galloped to Hanover to fetch them.

Ernst August looked splendid in his pleated leather traveling coat, his wide-topped boots and elegant breeches. He wore a fine wig and carried his three-cornered hat under his arm as he walked in, head high, with an assured and majestic stride. Trailing him, his son, the heir apparent, looked embarrassed and sulky.

George Louis charmed no one. He had already displeased Princess Anne, who had subsequently become Queen of England, and he would displease Sophia Dorothea. He was a clumsy, earthy man without taste or sensibility. He lived only for war or for its cousin, hunting. The great-grandson of James I of England, he was nonetheless the living contradiction of the traditional elegance and refinement of the Stuarts. An excellent and very brave soldier and essentially Germanic, he was the personification of force and cunning used for selfish ends. He had none of his mother's culture, no artistic taste except in music. His intelligence always served his own interests, and his sojourns at the courts of France and England had not improved his rough manners (even though, as the Princess Palatine put it, he had been "polished up" in Paris). Outwardly he was cold, reserved, phlegmatic, and sly. He was a short man, and his large and prominent blue eyes could be fierce, even cruel, as blue eyes sometimes are. His travels, far from contributing to his understanding of other countries, had made him even more contemptuous of foreigners. He was only happy in Germany. He had just spent two years in Venice, which had amused him as Italian comedy amused him. He imitated and envied France, but his resentment of the French grew out of his envy and mimicry.

During the introductions and embraces Princess Sophia suddenly lost her haughtiness and became gracious and affectionate. Then the question of the contract was broached.

The network of spies they had established in Celle kept the rulers of Hanover precisely informed about the Duke of Celle's fortunes, his numerous acquisitions, his estates, and Sophia Dorothea's wealth. This hoard was "a tidy sum to pocket," as Princess Sophia said later. And the Duke of Celle's weakness made the pocketing easy, for in his dynastic enthusiasm he granted all that was asked. He gave his daughter an income of 100,000 thalers a year, but this money went into the coffers of

Ernst August, and Sophia Dorothea would only see the crumbs that her father-in-law chose to leave her. Her estates were all signed into her husband's name. In the event of his death she would be entitled to a pittance of 12,000 thalers a year. While he lived, she was to receive nothing.

The richest heiress in Germany was henceforth penniless.

Eléonore was apparently not disturbed by this plundering of her daughter's fortune. On the other hand, she had insisted that Mme. de Busch, the mistress of George Louis, be banished from Hanover. Decidedly Eléonore had the soul of a provincial bourgeois.

Not without some embarrassment, Princess Sophia announced the engagement to the Princess Palatine in these words, and although today she was to welcome the union as a blessing, she would later condemn it as a misalliance: "One hundred thousand thalers is a tidy sum to pocket, to say nothing of a pretty girl who will have to deal with my son, the most pigheaded, stubborn boy I have ever seen. He has such a thick crust around his brains that I defy man or woman ever to discover what's inside. He does not care much for the match himself, but 100,000 thalers have tempted him, as they would have tempted anyone." This was the high-spirited tone of the most noble person in the milieu which Sophia Dorothea was about to enter. Like her mother, her future mother-in-law also spoke the language of a bourgeois, but a grasping and cynical one.

In fact, Eléonore was wrong to get upset about the Busch woman, who appeared to have little influence on George Louis. Much more formidable was Mme. de Busch's sister, the ambitious Baroness Platen, who ruled Ernst August's heart and who would play a disastrous role in Sophia Dorothea's life.

3 / Sophia Dorothea, Hereditary Princess

The marriage took place on November 21, 1682, in the chapel of the Castle of Celle. It was a beautiful sixteenth-century chapel whose elegance animated its Lutheran coldness. A massive central pillar of much earlier date supported a Gothic fan vault; the Apostles were naively represented along the balcony; the ducal pew overlooked a ladies' gallery that resembled a theater box with a grille. It was decorated with kneeling stools covered in crimson velvet and with small stools for the duchesses and folding chairs for the countesses. This exquisite chapel was to be the tomb of Sophia Dorothea's happiness.

A sinister light filtered through Renaissance windows that were overburdened with a thousand stained-glass coats of arms.

The young bride wore a crown made of sheets of silver and golden leaves, and her hair was hidden under a white velvet headband in the fashion of the country. She looked as though she were walking to the scaffold.

As the bells began to ring and the philosopher Leibnitz began to recite a poem composed for the occasion, a storm broke, as though nature were predicting the future. The whole district became enveloped in a thick fog, as warm air from the valley of the Rhine condensed on meeting the chilly wind from Scandinavia.

The night before, broken, defeated, and under obvious constraint, Sophia Dorothea had written the following letter to her aunt: "I have such great respect for my lord and master, the Duke, your husband, and for my lord and master, my own father, that however they choose to behave towards me I shall always be satisfied. Your Highness will, I know, do me the justice to believe that no one is more sensitive than I to all the proofs that She has given me of her kindness. I shall strive for the rest of my life to merit it so that Your Highness may be persuaded, by the respectful and humble way in which I shall serve Her, that She could not have chosen a daughter knowing better how to recognize her duties." (Celle, November 20, 1682.)

These articles of surrender, given by the victim to her executioner, were one of the horrible constraints imposed by social life and by the custom of the courts. One must not forget that these German princes were absolute sovereigns, rather like the Grand Moguls, not subject to popular opinion, having the right of life or death, only giving the appearance of liberalism for the benefit of the foreign envoys accredited to their courts.

The forbidding old palace at Hanover welcomed the young couple. The townsfolk, dressed in livery, lined the streets under triumphal arches. There were speeches, delegations, a presentation of the keys to the city amid streamers and flowers. Ernst August and Princess Sophia lived opposite in the castle bordering the Leine River.

Her Serene Highness, the hereditary Princess of Hanover, as Sophia Dorothea was henceforth called, found a household fully staffed with chamberlains, ladies in waiting, and pages. It was a house in which the strictest and most stifling ceremony prevailed.

The landscapes of Hanover are among the saddest and least colorful in Europe. After the dark forests of the Harz Mountains, the land slopes off to the dunes that border the North Sea, first as pasture land, next as peat bog, and finally as white sand. Farmhouses of blackish brick outlined with even darker half-timbering at the gables loom up from the meadows by the Leine or the Aller along with occasional clumps of lindens or birches. The breadth of the landscape reminds one of Prussia, while the colors are already those of Holland.

Sophia Dorothea looked at this uninspiring countryside and felt profoundly homesick. For her Celle was happiness itself, a charming Duchy, peaceful and slow-moving, with its Renaissance houses, their beams decorated with Gothic emblems and their double windows bright with geraniums; Celle with its ocher-colored castle fortified by four stout towers with sloping walls, its high roof topped by bronze bell towers that had oxidized green, and by gilded weather vanes; Celle where she had lived in her own apartments as a girl with her collection of delft china, her formal salon all crimson, her windows overlooking the lindens which dipped their branches into the moats and, at the end of the view, the horizon blocked by a forest of young pines.

Sophia Dorothea had brought her most treasured possessions to Hanover—her desk that had been fashioned from a piece of peasant furniture on skids, her childhood dolls, even her blue delft hens. She had also brought Eleonore de Knesebeck, who was almost exactly her age, as her maid of honor. Eleonore, the daughter of a Celle official, had left her family to follow Sophia Dorothea. Indeed, except for the loyal Eleonore and the common people, who would love the new bride at Hanover? George Louis was irreproachably and coldly polite to her. Sometimes she caught him looking at her strangely, almost as though he found her repulsive. No one could have been repelled by this lovely, elegant, and refined girl of sixteen. Without realizing it, George Louis was resurrecting the hatred, disgust, and contempt that, as a child, he had heard his mother lavish on Eléonore, "the little clot of dirt." Now he had been forced to marry the daughter of the "clot of dirt" for money. Unlike his father, who was avid for money, George Louis' passion was fighting. Now he was linked for life to this girl whom he could not help thinking of as tainted, and who, worst of all, would give him children tainted like herself with the same stigma of bastardy.

For her part, Sophia Dorothea did not forget the lessons she learned from Eléonore.

The two mothers bore a grave responsibility for the unhappiness of the young couple. For a long time they would try to advise, to calm, to appease, but it would be too late.

In Hanover, the days passed slowly for Sophia Dorothea. She spent much of her morning and even afternoon in bed; then she would go for a walk. At first she had ventured into town to do her errands, but she had had to give up these trips. Etiquette, on the model of that observed in Vienna, only sanctioned sorties in the gilded carriage drawn by six white Hanoverian horses. Sophia Dorothea would come home discouraged and bored and would go back to bed until it was time to dress, to deck herself out in jewels, and come down for the formal evening meal. It seemed to her that she had nothing else to do, and little by little she began to feel how irrelevant she was in this rigidly hierarchical court where people organized themselves in invisible, concentric circles. In first place were the marshals, in second the ministers, privy councillors, etc., and so on down to the last place occupied by the ushers, musicians, and doctors. Sophia Dorothea constantly made social blunders and was scolded by her mother-in-law, whose large flat cheeks would redden with displeasure. Princess Sophia tried her best to teach this ignorant little girl the subtleties of etiquette, but Sophia Dorothea's heart was not in it; it seemed to her that she had been wrenched out of a delicious dream and thrown into a bath of ice water. Her only desire was to rebel.

In the beginning she had made a few feeble efforts to win over a husband to whom she submitted without loving. She might perhaps have succeeded, for George Louis was not basically nasty. However, the scheming Baroness Platen pushed into his path a huge, soft, pink blonde named Ermengarde Mélusine von Schulenburg, with whom George Louis soon fell in love for life.

In this way Sophia Dorothea passed a rather dreary year. She did, however, bear a son, to the joy of all Hanover. The bride dried her tears, felt proud to be the hereditary Princess, and took pleasure in adorning herself for a brilliant court to which came distinguished guests, attracted by Princess Sophia's great friend, Leibnitz. She was happy too to be in high favor with her father-in-law. Always sensitive to feminine charms, the Duke of Hanover had been won over by the beauty, kindness, and sprightly spontaneity of his daughter-in-law. He felt a sincere affection for her and made many allowances for her.

Unfortunately, what should have been a good opportunity for Sophia Dorothea became the source of her
greatest misfortunes. Baroness Platen was already furious that this young beauty of infinitely higher rank had
replaced her as "the most beautiful lady in Hanover."
Now she was terrified at the thought that she might be
supplanted in the Duke's favors. To play this difficult
game, Sophia Dorothea would have needed the lucid
intelligence, the firmness, and the experience of her
mother-in-law. In fact she was simply sensitive and
affectionate, and lacked the intuition which is women's
salvation. She would have to defend herself without
help against the Baroness Platen, one of the worst harpies
the world has ever known.

Clara Elizabeth, Baroness Platen, was the daughter of
Count Philip von Meissenburg, a gentleman by rank, but
also a penniless military adventurer. At the time an
adventurer was not necessarily a crook, but often a
well-born young man in search of adventure. Clara
Elizabeth, her sister, Catherine Marie, and their father
traveled to seek their fortune. Palmblad says that they
arrived one day in Versailles where they met Mlle. de
Scudéry, and had even approached the King, to the fury
of Madame de Montespan. They failed in the same way
to reach King Charles II, for Madame de Kéroualle was
watching over him. Then they lowered their sights and
arrived, a little more experienced, at Osnabrück.[1] The
trio had fixed their sights on this little court that was so
well provided with young men. Their arrival coincided
with the return from abroad of George Louis and Frederick August, and their respective tutors Platen and
Busch. The fatted calf was killed in honor of the Prince

---

[1] W. F. Palmblad, *Aurora von Koenigsmark* (1853).

Bishop's two sons, and the von Meissenburg girls were invited to the party. They even acted in a French pastoral, astonishing the court by their beauty and their daring clothes. As shepherdesses they immediately found their sheep in the form of the two tutors. While George Louis returned to the army, Clara Elizabeth became Madame Platen[2] and Catherine Marie became Madame Busch.

Madame Platen was bolder and had fewer scruples than her sister. The two women accompanied their husbands when the latter followed Ernst August from Osnabrück to Hanover. For Madam Platen, the intriguer, her husband was only a steppingstone to the throne, and slowly, astutely, she set about winning over the Duke. Her success could be measured by her husband's promotion from tutor to privy councillor, and finally to prime minister. Madame Platen took advantage of these promotions to insinuate herself into Princess Sophia's intimate circle as a lady in waiting. The Princess closed her eyes to the liaison, which soon became semi-official, between Madame Platen and her husband. Her rank set her above such trifles, and moreover, Madame Platen treated her with the greatest respect. Having feathered her own nest, Madame Platen thought of her sister. After the father the son: Back from the army, George Louis soon fell into Madame Busch's net. He kept her as his mistress until his marriage.

Eléonore had insisted that Madame Busch be sent away, and Princess Sophia had given orders accordingly. During the wedding procession, therefore, she was furious to see the exile's face, convulsed with hate, staring

---

[2] "This woman, born of an illustrious house in Hesse, married Platen, a man of slight birth, but rich" (Anon. *Histoire Secrette*).

down from a window of the castle. Incensed that anyone would dare defy her, Princess Sophia sent word to Madame Busch to leave instantly, and the message was so worded that the concubine dared not show her face again. However, Madame Platen later contrived to bring her sister back and tried, unsuccessfully, to foist her onto a contemptuous George Louis. The historian Lewis Melville has affirmed that at this time George Louis was faithful to his wife.[3] This seems not to have been Sophia Dorothea's own opinion, because a strange contradiction in her character made her so furiously jealous of the husband she did not love that she made scenes and complained about him even to her parents-in-law.[4]

In 1685 the Duke of Hanover grew tired of these family conflicts and longed nostalgically for Venice and for his youth. After the marriage of his only daughter, Sophia Charlotte (an intelligent, cultivated, and calm girl, the portrait and the idol of her mother), to the Elector of Brandenburg, the Duke decided to return to Italy, accompanied by a large retinue.

The German princes, who were obsessed by the purity of blood in their marriages, cared nothing about it where their liaisons and their bastards were concerned. They sometimes ennobled their illegitimate children without, however, legitimizing them—the only point on which they failed to imitate Louis XIV. Like his royal model, the Duke was attached to his acknowledged mistress, Baroness Platen, whom he could not avoid taking with him to Venice.

---

[3] Lewis Melville, defender of George I to the detriment of his wife, implies (Vol. I, p. 57) that "Sophia Dorothea was an accomplished coquette."

[4] "The ladies had such a share in the government of Hanover that love was always mixed with affairs of state, and affairs of state with love. Nobody was idle, and everybody was constantly busy in pleasures and intrigues." (*Histoire Secrette*)

He lived there lavishly for two years. When he lacked money he had recourse to Hanover's principal export: his subjects. A fully equipped soldier was worth 15,000 pounds; six-footers were worth a lot more. When men were in short supply, press gangs carried them off from neighboring states. All the sovereigns did the same, from Prussia to Denmark. At the time of the coalitions, England financed a large proportion of the allied armies and sent only Irish or Scottish soldiers to Flanders or the Rhineland.[5] The Duke's stay in Venice was paid for by the sale to the Most Serene Public of 2,400 Hanoverian soldiers.[6] When he needed more money he used Sophia Dorothea's dowry.[7] Since it was only fair that she should have her share of it, and perhaps because he missed his pretty daughter-in-law, he sent one of his suite, General von Ilten, to bring her to Venice along with Mlle. de Knesebeck and von Ilten's wife, who was Grand Mistress of the court at Hanover.

Sophia Dorothea arrived in Venice at the beginning of 1684, just in time for carnival. The Duke arranged for her to be met at Mestre by a scarlet gondola manned by gondoliers dressed in crimson uniforms. Like the gondolas of all the great in Venice, his Serene Highness's were exempt from the law that required gondolas to be painted black.

Her stay in Venice was to be Sophia Dorothea's only great pleasure in these years. The Duke kept open house with four orchestras playing. Sophia Dorothea presided over a table at which the guests might be the Doge Morosini, in his horn-shaped hat of office, the state inquisitor, members of the powerful Council of

---

[5] *Memoires de la Margrave de Bayreuth.*
[6] Melville, *George I; op. cit.*
[7] W. H. Wilkins, *op. cit.*

Ten, and the Venetian nobility, not to mention all the great spies and small-fry informers of Europe. Sophia Dorothea and Countess Platen, who had declared a momentary truce, competed only for the grandeur of their gold brocade skirts, their velvet coats with long trains, and lace and jewels worth thousands of ducats.

In the course of these night-long revels, when Venice burned more candles than the rest of Italy put together, the two Hanoverian beauties, masked by their dominoes, would pass through the Piazza San Marco. Never had Sophia Dorothea been more beautiful. Her marvelous Nordic complexion had taken on a golden tinge. Compared to her freshness, the Platen woman seemed only a pale, or rather a blushing shadow because she painted her face in garish colors as was the fashion in Hanover. By some miracle she put up unflinchingly with the Princess's triumphs. For besides her beauty, Sophia Dorothea was a dancer without rival and an excellent musician. Being extremely cunning, the official mistress must have felt that it was better for the moment to let things ride, for the Duke was very proud of his daughter-in-law, and enchanted by her success. He was basically a kind man and he loved to see her enjoying herself with all the zest and enthusiasm of a child. Sophia Dorothea was fascinated by the tightrope walkers, the drawers of horoscopes, the acrobats who would slide down from the top of the Campanile, the marionettes, the jugglers. Everything delighted her: the regattas, the lottery, the ceremony of "wedding the sea," the gala balls of St. Moses, a visit to the latest palaces, such as the Pesaro or the Rezzonico, the snacks eaten in theater boxes after which one threw the chicken bones down into the pit. She would watch nuns take the veil, and battles in which flowers were the ammunition; she would lose her *zecchini* at the gaming tables, or watch the final work being done on the dome of the Salute.

On his return from Hungary, George Louis joined his family for a while in Venice, then went to Hanover while Sophia Dorothea, accompanied as always by the faithful Mlle. de Knesebeck, followed her father-in-law to Rome. There a small incident took place that her enemies did not fail to use against the young woman later. When George Louis arrived from Hungary, he was accompanied by a French comrade in arms, the Marquis de Lassaye, a sort of verbose Bussy-Rabutin, who seemed to have filled the courts of Europe with his gossip and his little plots. No sooner had the Marquis met Sophia Dorothea than he began to court her. He claimed that he wrote her thirteen very amorous letters couched in the high-flown style of the period. Fifty years later he published them in his *Memoirs,* a book printed in a very few copies on a press in his chateau. He waited until the Princess was dead, unable to defend herself, before implicating her in an intrigue that was obviously made up out of whole cloth. If he had written Sophia Dorothea, how is it that she did not reply and that he had not kept her answers rather than copies of his own letters, which he kept for fifty years? Conceit can sometimes turn a gentleman into something of a cad. Doubtless Melville was thinking of this story when he described Sophia Dorothea as a "perfect coquette." It is probable that the Princess was intially amused by the young Frenchman's wit and his tenacity, because her father-in-law appears to have told her that he had noticed them.

Her wonderful holiday over, the Princess returned to her monotonous existence in Hanover. She showed herself little in 1686 because she was pregnant and preparing for the birth of what turned out to be a daughter who was named Sophia Dorothea for her mother. The child was greeted with much less enthusiasm than her little brother had been. After all, who could have foreseen that the girl would one day be Queen of Prussia and mother of Frederick the Great?

The Duke had just elevated the Platen woman to the rank of Countess, as a favor to his minister, and the official mistress now no longer even tried to hide her hatred of the Princess. She had controlled it in Venice and Rome; in Hanover it overflowed. Her house became a hotbed of venomous intrigues nurtured against Sophia Dorothea. For Madame Platen no pretext was too futile to feed her hate. On one occasion the countess lingered longer than usual on her walk and arrived home to find the Duke already there in the garden exchanging banter with a pretty chambermaid named Ilse. Surprising them, the Countess took the incident as an affront and as soon as the Duke left she had the unfortunate Ilse thrown into prison. When the girl was set free a few months later, the Countess was still furious and ordered that Ilse be banished ignominiously from Hanover. The persecuted girl hit on the idea of seeking refuge in Celle, where the Duchess Eléonore took her in as her chambermaid. The Platen woman was deadly angry, not at Eléonore but at Sophia Dorothea, who had nothing to do with the matter. The shrewish Platen was so violent and so nasty that the Duke himself was afraid of her and constantly gave way to her. The young princes, George Louis' younger brothers, detested her and played tricks on her. One evening at supper, for example, they sprayed her with water, causing the rouge on her cheeks to dissolve and trickle in long driblets onto her ripening bosom. In her fury she had Prince Maximilian punished with unusual and excessive severity.

Madame Platen's vigilant hatred of Sophia Dorothea began to affect the young woman's relations with George Louis. When he caught measles, the Princess looked after him with such devotion that the atmosphere between husband and wife became more relaxed, and there was a semblance of friendship if not of love between them. But Madame Platen was hovering in the wings, and since George Louis would have nothing more to do with Madame de Busch, a new mistress had to be found for him. The wily Countess soon found just the person: Mlle. von Schulenburg, a huge, very beautiful young girl of noble birth but with no money. She invited the girl to her castle of Monplaisir, which the Duke had given her, and which was strategically situated between Leineschloss, where the Duke usually lived, and Herren-hausen, his summer house.

Invited to Monplaisir on his return from an expedition against the Turks, George Louis found himself constantly in the presence of Ermengarde Mélusine von Schulen-burg, a blonde Brünnhilde with cow eyes. Like all short men, he liked very tall women, and so fell into this gigantic trap. He immediately took her up and was seen with her quite openly at the theater and at the hunt. Soon he could not do without Mélusine.

Sophia Dorothea, indignant at her husband's new infidelity, complained first to her parents-in-law, then to her parents. All of them wisely advised her to turn a blind eye to the affair.

Venice seemed so far away. . . . Her memory of it was vanishing in the thick mists of the low Hanover sky that was broken only by V formations of wild geese flying over the Weser and the Elbe. The rivers flowed through fields of sparse buckwheat and red cabbages, their waters greenish where they were not soaked up by bogs and sand banks. Jean Baptiste Tavernier, the celebrated seventeenth-century French Huguenot traveler, has left a description of this Hanover where he stopped on his way to Amsterdam. Days of hunting for heron or wild boar and hours at table were followed by evenings spent with generals in smoke-filled rooms, and performances of boring German comedies alternating with plays given by the French drama troupe, concerts on the hydraulic organ, sled races, parades, the changing of the guard to the sounds of fife and drum, reviews of the military in battle order, frequent cannon salvos honoring foreign princes, and then tables laid for a hundred with golden dishes and goblets.[8]

Sophia Dorothea felt immensely weary, morally as well as physically, during her daily after-dinner walks along the arrow-straight paths at Herrenhausen. Her lively mind and her charming wit were becoming dulled as she strolled between the walls of funereal box and trimmed hedges beside her mother-in-law, that indefatigable walker whose long stride wore out everyone. Here no one's sensibility spoke to the soul, and that was the only language that Sophia Dorothea understood. Princess Sophia spoke only of protocol and precedence. She was concerned only with the diplomatic quarrels between the envoys of France and England, always at daggers-drawn in their rivalry for influence at Hanover. The young woman had to endure long courses in English history because Princess Sophia, tremendously proud of her Stuart blood, lived with her eyes fixed on London. Sophia Dorothea ended up knowing by heart each of the colored stone walks, each grove, each crossroad, each

---

[8] *J. B. Tavernier*, by Charles Joret (Paris, 1886).

patch of lawn. Everything was clipped in ball shapes and the fortifications of previous centuries were laid out as flowerbeds. The old sentry boxes had become niches for statues of Flora and Zephyrus, and the grenadiers constantly on guard in front of the palace were actually box trees trimmed in the shape of grenadiers. They provided a setting for flowerbeds designed by Charbonnier, a pupil of Lenôtre's. The completely renovated palace gave evidence of recent embellishments for which Sophia Dorothea's dowry had helped to pay. Gilded lead statues glittered everywhere. The budget of Hanover continued to be regularly fed by the sale of recruits who rarely came back from war. (Thackeray says that only 1,400 of a contigent of 6,700 soldiers sent to the Peloponnesus came back.) While maintaining an army of 36,000 men himself, the Duke continued to sell soldiers to France, Prussia, Holland, and Spain. He sent them not only to the Emperor to protect Vienna, but as far as India in the service of the British East India Company. These foot soldiers served to pay for the silver bathtubs, the gondolas in the pond brought back from Venice, the jewels bought from Tavernier, in short, all the things that delighted Countess Platen and even Sophia Dorothea.

The hereditary princess was less fond of the old Gothic entertainments, some of which had fortunately been abandoned. They included throwing candy money at each other while at table, watching bulls with fireworks on their horns fight lions, or preventing deer in heat from mating. The meals, which sometimes lasted nine hours, were hateful. The merrymaking could include up to three thousand toasts drunk in round-bottomed glasses that could not be put down unless they had been drained. The china would be broken at dessert and dancing would begin on tables strewn with dishes and platters accompanied by somersaulting dwarfs and the buffooneries of jesters.

At least these vulgar pleasures radiated gaiety, good health, and a robust love of life. Much more refined and infinitely dismal were the soirees given by Princess Sophia. The Princess was difficult to deal with, and when she had had her fill of striding along the garden paths, she would write to the whole of Europe, and above all to her beloved niece, the Princess Palatine, who was the sister-in-law of Louis XIV. These two ladies had the wit and temperament of men, and on occasion could joke like troopers. The evidence is in two famous and incredibly crude letters that these noble ladies exchanged.[9] The Duke read his regular and his deciphered correspondence in his secret study, paying particular attention to the dispatches of the College of the Princes of the Empire. The College was violently opposed to the creation of a ninth electorate which Ernst August, advised by his wife, so ardently desired.

If one were to ignore Princess Sophia's hateful haughtiness, cruelty, and cynicism toward her sister-in-law of Celle, one could admire her as a most remarkable woman. As intelligent as she was cultivated, she spoke and wrote five languages and was versed in the sciences and in philosophy. The greatest minds of Germany enjoyed talking with her, and Leibnitz, who had settled in Hanover, was totally devoted to her. She had a remarkable political flair, was most useful to her husband in his ambition to gain the electorate. While in London she cleverly strengthened his chances of sitting on the throne of England, which was her dream. Having married

---

[9] See the famous letter: "I do not shit comfortably when my ass is in midair. . . ." (Fontainebleau, October 9, 1694). And Princess Sophia's answer (Hanover, October 31, 1694).

without love (for she preferred and would always prefer George Wilhelm of Celle to Ernst August), she was nonetheless a faithful wife and when George Wilhelm began to regret his decision and pay her court, she dryly put him in his place. She gave her husband five princes, and while she never liked the eldest, she adored the four others, who were taken from her one after another to be sent into exile or to be killed in wars. She almost died of grief when she heard of the death of her favorite. On this point she might have found some common ground with Sophia Dorothea who was very fond of her young brothers-in-law. But grief did not bring them together. Princess Sophia had not been brought up to show her sorrow.

Evenings at the castle were joyless. There were sober card parties of basset, omber, and faro, a little music, a little conversation with foreign representatives, secret agents, and distinguished visitors. The young courtiers in search of amusement would excuse themselves and dash to Monplaisir, the Countess Platen's charming castle, where they would dance, gamble for high stakes, and drink until morning.

Sophia Dorothea saw before her only a road that led nowhere. She would fall asleep listening to the beating of her lonely heart.

4 / The Rosenkavalier

Mlle. de Knesebeck affirmed that Sophia Dorothea and the Count of Königsmark had known and loved each other in their childhood. And although this has been contested in a number of biographies, its truth was definitively established by a letter of September 16, 1692.[1]

They looked alike: they had the same lion's mane of mahogany-colored hair, delicate features, and unrivaled grace. Both were implusive, passionate, reckless, and generous. She was the friend of the poor; he the idol of his soldiers.

Philipp Christoph, Count of Westerwyk and Steghorn, Count of Königsmark, was the second son of General Königsmark, a celebrated warrior who was killed at the siege of Bonn. His elder brother, Karl Hans, after a series of extraordinary adventures, died in the Peloponnesus, that tomb of so many German recruits. One of his two sisters became the Countess of Loewenhaupt; the other was the famous Aurora, a great European beauty, who never married.

Königsmark, having met Prince August of Saxony, accompanied him on his travels to Spain, Portugal, and Italy. Nothing more is known about him until 1681,

---

[1] On that date Königsmark wrote to Sophia Dorothea that he had loved her since the day he first saw her and that he had not declared himself only because he was too much of a child to dare speak.

when he left Sweden, where his father commanded Charles XI's artillery. In that year he and his brother, Karl Hans, sailed from Gothenburg for Hull and England. Furnished with a letter of introduction to Charles II, Karl Hans came to seek his fortune in London, while his younger brother was to learn fencing at the academy run by Major Fulbert, and then prepare for entrance to Cambridge University. The king took a great liking to this charming Karl Hans, who was also feted by the entire English nobility. The young man was related to three royal families and had the means to put on a show that befitted his rank.

Contemporaries' English memoirs and later Moreri in his *Historical Dictionary*, and Palmblad (not to mention Horace Walpole, who in his *Reminiscences* confuses the two brothers) have left us a thousand details about this extravagant character. Karl Hans was the very prototype of the adventurer in a time which knew so many bizarre heroes who resembled neither the Reiters[2] of the sixteenth century nor the sharpers of the eighteenth. These were men whose health, audacity, and immorality were equal to anything. Born in Fioni, Karl Hans visited England for the first time in 1674. Later he went to Paris where his uncle, William Othon, was a field marshal[3] in the army of the King of France (before becoming governor of Swedish Pomerania). In 1677 Karl Hans was called to arms in Italy. On his way there, accompanied by his mistress dressed as a page, he stopped at Chambéry. Taking a look around town, he returned to the inn to be met by the innkeeper crying: "My Lord, your page is having a baby!" From Italy he went to Malta

---

[2] The Reiters were German cavalry soldiers in the service of the Huguenots. — Trans.
[3] Equivalent of a brigadier general.

to fight the Turks. During a sea battle he fell into the water from his galley, was fished out again, and returned to Malta. There, although a Lutheran, he served for a time in the ranks of the Knights of Malta. He then fell ill, returned to France, and was put in charge of the Furstenberg regiment by Louis XIV. He was wounded at Kortriji, and had barely recovered before he went to fight in Catalonia. Finding himself in Spain in 1619 without more serious dangers to confront, he became noted for his skill in the bullring and to the "olés" of the senõras he was gored by a bull. Then he went to Portugal and was later seen in Paris, Holland, Hamburg, and Sweden.

The Königsmarks were attracted by heiresses, and in London Karl Hans met one of England's richest widows—Countess Ogle, the orphaned daughter of the eleventh Earl of Northumberland (whose fortune is still immense today). At the age of eleven this very much sought after girl had married the Earl of Ogle, the son of the Duke of Newcastle. Widowed a year later, the rather pretty redheaded Elizabeth, still only a debutante, was all the rage in London. She was nicknamed the Sad Heiress and also Countess Carrot. Karl Hans proved most attentive and entered the lists, but met the customary British diffidence toward foreign suitors, even Nordic ones.

Rejected and disappointed, Königsmark rushed off to fight in Algiers. In 1681, at the siege of Tangiers, his horse was killed under him. He crossed the Straits again and boarded a ship of the British fleet at Gibraltar, accompanied by one of his comrades, a Swedish Captain Vraatz, and was back in London in 1682.

There he found that his beloved Countess Ogle had been married by her prudent family to "a young blood" named Thomas Thynne, who was so rich that he was nicknamed Ten Thousand Tom, an allusion to his 10,000 pounds of income.[4] Her husband was impotent, so Mrs. Thynne, at the age of fourteen, fled to Holland the day after the wedding. Königsmark felt that the moment had come to court her again. The only obstacle was Thynne, a celebrated young man around London, one of Dryden's heroes, and a rakehell.

Still accompanied by Captain Vraatz, Königsmark went to ground in his London lodgings, pretending that he had caught a skin disease in Morocco. Vraatz, a tremendous fighter, tried to provoke Thynne to a duel, but Thynne evaded him. At this moment a Pole named Boroski arrived from Sweden, bringing a fresh supply of horses for Königsmark's stables. As Thynne obstinately refused to respond to the challenge, Vraatz armed the Pole and a Lieutenant Stein. According to one version of the story, these two hired assassins ambushed Thynne as he came out of Pall Mall and brought him down with a pistol shot. He died three hours later. According to another version, a duel took place and Boroski, as one of the seconds, killed Thynne. London was up in arms, and all three men were thrown in jail, where Karl Hans Königsmark joined them shortly as an accomplice, for arms had been found in his house. Philipp Christoph bravely came to London to testify in his elder brother's behalf. In February 1682, the guilty parties were sentenced to be hanged. As he went to the scaffold, Vraatz had this final word: "I hope God will behave like a gentleman to me." Only Königsmark escaped the law, thanks to the intervention of Charles II. To avoid scandal, the twice-widowed Mrs. Thynne married Charles Seymour, the sixth Duke of Somerset. London

---

[4] W. Boulton. *In the Days of the Georges*, 1909.

had become impossible for Karl Hans, who turned up subsequently in Flanders, then at the siege of Verona, and finally in the Peloponnesus. He died before Pylos, sick and exhausted.

On his death his younger brother, Philipp Christoph, became Count of Königsmark.

Supremely handsome, noble, brave, and rich, the new Count's prospects appeared to be limitless. Versailles, Vienna, The Hague, and Madrid beckoned to him. But he preferred little Hanover to them all.

In 1684 the *Mercure Galant* noted: "The Court of Hanover, which follows all the manners of the French court, also imitates it in its entertainments." Toland wrote that no German court could be compared to Hanover's: No one got drunk there, and distinguished foreigners who were invited to dine with the Elector were surprised by the atmosphere of good breeding that prevailed at his table. The palace on the Leine had just been restored and included a theater with sixty boxes, with the Countess Platen's facing the one belonging to the Electress. Toland added that no entrance fee was charged, for all expenses of the theater were borne by the Prince. As for the audience, Lady Mary Wortley Montagu wrote in 1716: "All the Hanoverian ladies have cheeks that are literally rose colored, snowy-white foreheads and bosoms, jet-black eyebrows, blood-red lips, and hair as black as coal. They maintain this perfection until they die and they look wonderful by candlelight. Amid such beauty only variety is lacking. All the ladies look alike, as do the ladies of the English court shown in Mrs. Salmon's wax museum in London. Touch them to a flame and they would melt. . . ."

We are far from the primitive manners of the beginning of the seventeenth century, thirty years earlier. France and the Holy Roman Empire frantically outbid each other distributing pensions to the German princes while the envoys of both powers tried to make their influence felt to the detriment of their colleagues by giving ever more magnificent presents.

Travelers all praised the extreme courtesy with which they were welcomed at Hanover. J. B. Tavernier described life at Herrenhausen where the Elector spent his mornings in the chapel and his afternoons in the theater, to be entertained by his own troupe of French actors. The jeweler Tavernier left Hanover in a court carriage, all his expenses having been paid, taking with him a silver ewer that had been given him as a farewell present.

According to the *Mémoires* of Malortie, the most accurate of his chroniclers, Philipp Christoph von Königsmark arrived in Hanover on March 11, 1688. That same evening he attended a ball at the old castle and his entrance was immediately noticed. He greeted the hereditary Prince and, bowing low before the hereditary Princess, murmured: "Does Your Serene Highness remember that I was her page at the Court of Celle?" Sophia Dorothea remained silent: She was moved by everything that reminded her of that lost paradise of her youth. She smiled. Königsmark was welcome, and not only to her. Ernst August named him colonel of the guard, a position which brought him only a modest salary[5] but which put him in the third rank of the court hierarchy. The young princes were delighted with this handsome man who was both a courtier and a soldier. In fact, he was above all a great adventurer. Enjoying himself, flirting, and fighting were his life. He was an excellent lover and

---

[5] The author of the *Histoire Secrète* said "with a large pension."

that supremely seventeenth-century noun "gallantry" seemed to have been coined for him. He was thirty; Sophia twenty-four. They met at a masked ball.

Königsmark and misfortune were masked when they entered Sophia Dorothea's life.

The hereditary Princess was not well at the time and seldom went out. Her young brothers-in-law would bring Königsmark to her salon in the evening, where they all met before dutifully going down to Princess Sophia's dull soirees. They made the nucleus of an opposition. The law of primogeniture which Ernst August was relentlessly trying to establish (for he thought it would bring him more quickly to the electorate) favored the eldest son to the serious detriment of the younger sons, who began to think of revolt. For the moment they were still just grumbling. Sophia Dorothea had grounds for complaint too. George Louis was constantly seen with Mélusine, and Sophia Dorothea, mocking and sharp, openly made fun of the couple, which annoyed her husband even more. Neglected and her pride hurt, Sophia Dorothea complained to her parents-in-law. As a result, George Louis behaved brutally toward her. A visit to Hanover by the Duke and Duchess of Celle did not help. At a grand costume ball given in their honor, Sophia Dorothea, as a beautiful Flora, danced a minuet with Königsmark, who was dressed in rose and silver brocade. Their performance captivated everyone . . . and unfortunately maddened Countess Platen. She could no longer control herself. She must have this Königsmark; she must take this Rosenkavalier from Sophia Dorothea. The anonymous author of the *Histoire secrette de la duchesse de Hanover* (*Secret History of the Duchess of Hanover*) states plainly: "As he received the frontal assault of Countess Platen's compliments,

Königsmark understood the real meaning of what she was saying. Despite his passion for the Princess, he was not insensible to the advances of a woman as beautiful as the Countess. He replied that he was unworthy of this attention, but that since she would allow him to seek her out that very evening. . . ." When Königsmark visited the Countess he found her in a negligee, reclining on a sofa. Abandoning all modesty, she rushed to embrace him, confessed her weakness for him, and allowed him to see so many of her charms that Königsmark did not hesitate to respond to her show of affection. It was almost dawn before he retired to his own room. He tried in vain to sleep, but he continually reproached himself for having succumbed to the charms of the Princess's enemy. The incident was reported to Sophia Dorothea, who was deeply hurt and felt that she had been abandoned—the more so as she had just had a bad fight with her husband. George Louis had changed a great deal under the influence of Mélusine and, through her, of Countess Platen.

In his youth he had been a model of virtue and good behavior, even a prig. That he did not fit into his father's frivolous court is revealed by two incidents. Once in Osnabrück he was reviewing a parade of veterans who had fought bravely under his command against the Turks in Hungary. The young Prince was indignant to see tacked on to the end of this parade two unknown ladies, the Mlles. Meissenburg, masquerading rather more undressed than dressed as Bellona and Diana. As previously noted, these young ladies became Countess Platen and Madame de Busch. The other incident is more important and almost ended badly, for the Elector, who was so indulgent with others, was very strict with his sons. At a court banquet the Elector offered a toast in a goblet which the guests realized with horror was a chalice. The Elector offered the cup to his son George Louis, who not only refused to touch it, but sharply rebuked his father. The latter flushed with anger, but then having gathered from the murmurs around the table that the diners sided with George Louis, he laughed the whole thing off.

Madame Platen, seeking to become as influential with the son as with the father, tried to tempt George Louis with her sister, Madame de Busch, but he rejected her with contempt. However, Platen always got what she wanted. It is not known how she did it, but the fact is that George Louis one day found himself in love with Mélusine von Schulenburg. It was because of the enormous blonde that George Louis and his wife had the famous quarrel mentioned by the chroniclers and described in detail by Palmblad. One evening while returning to her own apartments from a soiree at her mother-in-law's, Sophia Dorothea lost her way in the ill-lit corridors of the palace. She and her ladies in waiting, Mlle. de Knesebeck and Mme. Sansdorf, arrived in front of a door which the Princess ordered them to open. Mlle. de Knesebeck went in first and immediately dashed out again; Mme. Sansdorf did the same, and both ladies tried to dissuade the Princess from entering. She would not listen to them and entered what turned out to be a bedroom where a very pale young woman was lying on the bed with a newborn baby in a cradle by her side. A man was holding her hand, and the Princess recognized him as her husband. Sophia Dorothea immediately began to denounce him with great violence. At first the Prince was sheepish, but when he saw that the young mother had fainted from terror, he became enraged and, throwing himself on his wife, seized her by the throat.

He would have strangled her despite the cries of the growing audience if he had not remembered the prophecy that a clairvoyant had once made: "If you kill her you will die . . . the following year."

Sophia Dorothea complained in vain to her parents-in-law and asked them to banish Mélusine. But the Electress replied coldly that she was not accustomed to concern herself with such stupidities. As for the Elector, he tried to console Sophia, advising her to close her eyes to a kind of adventure common in all courts, and even implying that she had been imprudent in her dealings with Königsmark. . . .

To judge by the short, platonic, respectful, and tender letters of this period, Königsmark was not yet the Princess's lover. He had promised to serve her body and soul. It was for her that he lingered in Hanover, neglecting his own interests and his future. He had begun by evoking memories of their childhood romance, their races around the castle's frozen moats, he dutifully pushed the sled in which his little idol sat bundled up, warming a tiny dog in her muff. He recalled the promises they traced with their fingers on the castle's 383 moist windows: "Forget me not . . . forget me not."

He had not forgotten, and he wanted to avenge her for the misconduct of her husband. With magnificent recklessness, he planned to challenge George Louis to a duel, and kill him or die.

Meanwhile, despite his remorse, he returned to Madame Platen's. When Sophia Dorothea reproached him, he replied that he did it to conceal his real feelings from people, and that, after all, Madame Platen was pursuing him only to ensure a good match for her daughter (whose father was rumored to be Duke Ernst August). The little court, constantly watching new arrivals and always eavesdropping on the most trifling gossip, counted the evenings he passed at Monplaisir. Frivolous and pleasure-loving, Königsmark did not resist the attractions of this Abbaye de Thélème[6] at the heart of the immense tedium of Hanover, where everything was Baroque, from furniture to morals. At Monplaisir, Madame Platen had created a sort of club for bachelors where she wished to see no woman except herself. Königsmark gambled, danced, and drank there a great deal.[7]

There was an interlude during which Königsmark went to Venice to bury his old uncle and come into his property. He reached the height of opulence, for he inherited from his father, his brother, and his uncle. Having bought a property close to Hamburg, he returned to Hanover and went on a wild spending spree. This was in 1689. He had first come to Hanover in March, 1688.[8]

The Count settled down to a sumptuous life. His house was situated on the edge of the Duke's park, and he had only to cross a corner of the garden to be under Sophia Dorothea's windows. According to his secretary's account book, he had at this time twenty-nine servants and fifty-two horses.

He dazzled the duchy, but not Sophia Dorothea. He was one of her intimates and she treated him as a devoted friend, nothing more. He, on the other hand, was madly

---

[6] Abbaye de Thélème, Liberty Hall, as described in Rabelais' *Gargantua.* — Trans.

[7] Anonymous. *Histoire Secrette.*

[8] Palmblad says that Königsmark arrived in 1683, which is significant. Sophia Dorothea's daughter, the future Queen of Prussia and mother of Frederick the Great, was born in 1686. According to Palmblad's hypothesis, she could have been Königsmark's daughter. Thus the royal house of Prussia would have the blood of the Königsmarks, not the Guelphs, running in its veins. However, as Palmblad hated Prussia, there is no reason to accept his dates, which are contradicted by a serious witness, Malortie.

in love, probably from the first day. Otherwise it is hard to explain why he stayed on at Hanover, refusing a number of brilliant offers, neglecting his career, his future, his happiness. He was unhappy and was dying to leave, torn as he was between his adoration for the Princess and the tribute that Madame Platen demanded. To escape these emotional complications, he asked to be part of the expeditionary force that the Duke sent to the Peloponnesus in January 1690 under the leadership of his twenty-one-year-old son, Charles. In all fairness to these German princes, it must be said that while they trafficked in the lives of their subjects, they did not hesitate to risk those of their sons and sometimes their own. The Balkan adventure was an appalling disaster; at Priština, in what is now Yugoslavia, the Hanoverians were cut to pieces by the scimitars of the Turks. The body of poor little Prince Charles was found under a heap of corpses of the officers who had tried to defend him. When the news reached Hanover, there was general mourning. The Prince was loved by everyone, adored by his mother, and a dear friend of Sophia Dorothea's. The Duchess Sophia became so gravely ill that she had to be sent to Carlsbad to take the waters.

Königsmark was thought to be among the dead, but he had the nine lives of all the Königsmarks, and he returned to Hanover in April bringing with him the few sad survivors of the massacre at Priština. The Wolfenbüttel contingent alone, 11,000 strong at the outset, had been reduced to 130 men.

It was about this time that Königsmark and Sophia Dorothea began to write to each other—or at least it is from this period that their surviving correspondence dates. They do not appear to have written to one another previously. Königsmark was ill with malaria that he had contracted in the Balkans, and he begged Sophia Dorothea to bring him back to life by sending him a word of friendship. "I am on the verge of death now," he wrote, "and the only thing that can save me is a word from the incomparable princess," whose slave he declared himself to be.

Lightly and without foresight, he provoked the birth of a correspondence which would be fatal to both of them.

Königsmark received the word on which he said his life depended. But he would never be content. He had an impetuous, violent, jealous temperament, hungry for love and for kisses. He was a spoiled child, a chatterbox, a boaster, a drinker, a flirt, forever unsatisfied. The more he received the more he asked for, and in a more and more peremptory manner. He demanded, he begged, and he threatened. His strategy as a lover was faultless. He caressed and cajoled the anxious creature he desired, then aroused her with jealous accusations. He did not play fair, for it is too easy to terrify a woman in love by threatening either to leave immediately or to go and get oneself blown up in battle.

Their romance took place against a backdrop of battles, sieges, and entrenchments: Mons, Steenkerke, Halle. . . . After tortuous negotiations and bargaining worthy of a horse-trader, Ernst August, always pursuing the Electorate, entered the Grand Alliance against Louis XIV. The leaders of the coalition met at The Hague: The republican city became a city of kings. There were the Emperor Leopold, the kings of Spain, Poland, Denmark, and Sweden, the dukes of Savoy and Brunswick, the princes of Saxony and Nassau, the regent of Württemberg, the electors of Brandenburg and Bavaria. . . . There was feasting and banqueting as there would be later at the Congress of Vienna. Meanwhile, Louis XIV took Mons. The unexpected stroke dispersed the gathering, and Ernst August returned to Hanover, taking König-smark with him.

Philipp Christoph was once more only a few hundred yards from his idol. But was he happy? Not in the least. Although he had no claim on her, he never stopped reproaching her, as though she were already his.

"After what you have done to me, must I still love you? Still, your disdainful manner has made me decide to leave the day after tomorrow. If you still wish to comfort a poor heart eaten up with jealousy, let me come you know where. . . . This is perhaps the only favor that I shall ask of you, because I hope that the good Lord will take me from this world rather than make me suffer in this way. So I beg of you do not refuse me."

And in the following letter:

"I am in utter despair to find so few chances to speak to you. I hardly dare admire the eyes which give me life. Please, allow me to find the means to say two words to you! I shall leave the day after tomorrow. God knows when I shall see my life, my goddess, again. The thought is death to me."

Apparently he did not know, or did not wish to know, to what point each of their gestures was spied on and criticized in this little court. Nevertheless, an incident that occurred on his return from the Peloponnesus should have put him on guard. Even then, as one of the Princess's intimates, he would walk with her in the park and play with her children. One day her little daughter, being tired, asked Königsmark to take her back to the palace. He carried her in his arms to her apartments, which was contrary to protocol: The governess or a gentle-man in waiting should have been called. Madame

Platen kicked up such a fuss that the Duke was annoyed when he heard about the incident.

About the same time, Madame Platen organized a malicious intrigue that was to have unpleasant consequences. Königsmark gave a grand masked costume ball at which all the court and high officials were presented. Sophia Dorothea was wearing a brocaded pink dress and a pair of initialed and embroidered gloves that her husband had brought back to her from The Hague. Platen stole one of the gloves and at the height of the ball persuaded Königsmark to come into the garden with her on this lovely summer's night. She was looking extremely beautiful and was dressed in pink like the Princess. She made such passionate advances to the frivolous Königsmark that he could not help kissing her and holding her in his arms. As a result he failed to hear the approach of George Louis, who was being led by at the crucial moment by Count Platen, as arranged beforehand between the Count and Countess. Pretending to be frightened, the Countess fled from Königsmark, after dropping the stolen glove. Platen picked it up and handed it to George Louis. In the dark the Prince had seen only a woman dressed in pink. . . . He immediately recognized the glove and, when he returned to the salon he heard Sophia Dorothea complain of having lost it. The intrigue was well arranged to arouse suspicions in the mind of George Louis who, until then, had never doubted his wife's faithfulness.

This clever plot, which Victorien Sardou would have envied, is related in the apocryphal *Mémoires*, but it is possible that it was based on a real incident. Madame Platen's influence and insolence were growing by the minute. From Baroness she had risen to Countess, and her jewels outshone Sophia Dorothea's. Obsequious

62

with Duchess Sophia (who was unusually obliging), she was irritatingly offhand and patronizing with Sophia Dorothea, thus wounding the Princess's pride.

True or false, the story of the glove throws a curious light on the state of people's minds in Hanover. They were most preoccupied with the relationship that was developing or might develop between the hereditary Princess and the colonel of the guards. Not only were Madame Platen, Mélusine Schulenburg, and the whole court actively interested in this romance, but Duchess Sophia herself began to be worried and made a show of praising Königsmark to her daughter-in-law in order to observe her reaction. When the Duchess visited Celle (for contact between the two courts was frequent and friendly) she would take Sophia Dorothea with her daily on the interminable loping walks that exhausted her retinue, and she would recount to her at length the history of that England over which she would be called on to reign. Like a sleepwalker, obsessed only by the thought of Königsmark, Sophia Dorothea did not even try to feign interest.

The undeniably able German scholar Georg Schnath has dated all the letters that passed between the lovers by comparing the circumstances within them and con- temporary events. Thanks to him, it is possible to fix the month in which Sophia Dorothea yielded to Königs- mark's entreaties. The first letter was written in July 1690, and until the following April they all ended in the respectful manner proper for a colonel of the guards writing to the hereditary Princess. But on April 30, 1691, the tone changed and "your faithful servant" be- came "farewell by beloved brunette, I embrace your knees."

The first letters were sealed with the image of a heart

on an altar lit by a ray of sunlight and the motto: "Nothing impure can set me on fire." Later Königsmark used another seal showing two hearts, one enclosed in the other and the surrounding motto: *"Cosi fosse il vostro dentro il mio"* ("Thus might yours be inside mine").

The motto became a fact. Sophia Dorothea no longer ruled her own heart. If Duchess Sophia still had only very vague suspicions,[9] Duchess Eléonore was extremely worried. Gently and cautiously the mother tried to warn the daughter to be careful. Königsmark felt it and immediately became frantic. His love affairs were not in very good shape. He was madly in love with this woman, but he never saw her. He imagined her surrounded by suitors, and felt that his enemies were undermining him. It was a difficult year; it was the year of the Flanders campaign and there were endless battles. . . .

In July 1692 Duke Ernst August achieved his lifelong goal. He became Elector of Hanover. Princess Sophia became the Electress, George Louis the Electoral Prince, and Sophia Dorothea the Electoral Princess. The Elector had become a person of importance on the European level; his son George Louis commanded an allied army in Flanders.

There were splendid festivities in Hanover to celebrate these great events. Among other attractions, Ernst August brought in an Italian theater company "superior to anything seen at Versailles." The guests flocked in, and the Duke and Duchess of Celle were welcomed more warmly than any.

But all hearts were not at peace, even in the midst of the rejoicing. The Duke, who was basically a kind man,

[9] She did not suspect that the eventuality she feared had become a reality almost a year before.

was unhappy because he had had to execute Count von Moltke and exile Prince Maximilian. The latter, incensed by the law of primogeniture, had plotted against his father with Moltke and the inevitable Anthony Ulrich von Wolfenbüttel, always the enemy of Ernst August and his policies. The Electress was still disconsolate about the loss of her two young sons, Charles and Christian, whom the war had taken from her. George Louis was preoccupied with his campaign in Flanders where, the following month, he would fight the bloody and indecisive battle of Steenkerke that would leave 14,000 men dead. Sophia Dorothea thought anxiously of the letter she would write to Königsmark to forestall his continual complaints that she was an unfaithful coquette. Only the Duke of Celle was truly happy. His brother had succeeded; Hanover had become an Electorate, and on the death of Ernst August the three Hanoverian states, the old Guelph appanage, would become one of the most important countries of the Empire. His daughter seemed to be on good terms with her husband ever since she had devotedly nursed him through the attack of measles that he had brought back from the front. Only Eléonore d'Olbreuse was farsighted enough to shudder at the thought of the evil that could result from Königsmark's wild passion—"this man born to create great disorders," as Saint-Simon said.

It is probable that from 1692 on some of Königsmark's letters were intercepted and read in the Duke's secret study, because in that year Ernst August's attitude began to change. Before that Königsmark had been in the Duke's good graces. In July 1691 he was entrusted with a confidential mission to Hamburg, where he had property, to work toward an alliance between Hanover and Sweden. It was an unfortunate choice of negotiators because Charles XI of Sweden hated his subjects to leave their country and serve foreigners. Königsmark came back empty-handed, but as usual he was well-received on his return.

In 1692 the atmosphere changed, and Königsmark felt it. First he was refused leave to go to Hanover. But he absolutely had to see Sophia Dorothea; their lives had become an intricate torture. He was with the army at Ath, Eppendorf, Dist, Namur; she was with her parents or parents-in-law at Wienhausen or at Celle, at Luisburg or Brockhausen. . . . She was eating her heart out because her lover was at war; he was frantic with jealousy because she shone at court, surrounded by suitors, according to him. They wrote each other constantly, and although there were excellent reasons why their letters might be lost or arrive late, every delay sent them into fits of anguish or suspicion.

At the end of the campaign of 1692, Königsmark, a colonel of the guards, again asked for a pass to return to Hanover. He was refused and sent instead to Dist, where the army was preparing to go into winter quarters. With his habitual rashness and disdain for the consequences of his actions, he feigned sickness, rushed to Hanover in disguise, and went straight to the apartments of the hereditary Princess. The next day, a little worried, he presented himself to Marshal Podewils, who received him coldly. Podewils was a Pomeranian who had taken service in France, but being a Huguenot, the revocation of the Edict of Nantes had obliged him to return to his own country. Then he went into the service of Hanover. A friend of Eleonore of Celle and of Philipp Christoph, he was usually inclined to help. But this time he was reticent, for he had just finished an unpleasant job. He had been charged by the Duke to make Aurora von

Königsmark understand that she had ceased to be *persona grata* and that he wished her to leave Hanover forever. Aurora kept house for her brother and from time to time acted as a letterbox for him. It was a serious insult to the Königsmark family, but Philipp Christoph dared not protest. His always tactful sister, sensing that Madame Platen had had a hand in her disgrace, pretended that she had been called to Hamburg on personal business and left quietly.

The "good man," as Podewils is called in the letters, had a good heart and he found a pretext to keep Königsmark in Hanover until autumn.

Still the lovers were not really happy. Never had they seen each other so little and with less satisfaction. Knowing that they were being spied on, they hardly dared exchange glances at the Electoress's receptions. Königsmark would fail to understand, or misinterpret, the signals made to him surreptitiously by Mlle. de Knesebeck, and whenever he failed to find hidden in his hat the letter he was expecting, he imagined that he had been betrayed.

With the approach of the festivities planned to celebrate the elevation of the Duke to the Electorate, Königsmark was obliged to depart. He did not take part in the battle of Steenkerke, remaining instead at Hamburg, where he was kept in the event that Hanover should go to war against the Danes. The coalitions that characterized this era fluctuated like the stock market. In strategic terms this meant interminable sieges, marches and counter-marches, and prolonged winter quarters.

Königsmark could bear it no longer. Invoking his double command, he hastened to join Sophia Dorothea at her parents in Celle. Duchess Eléonore, exasperated and frightened, spoke so seriously to her daughter that

Sophia Dorothea promised to make Königsmark leave. He feigned obedience and announced his departure for the Peloponnesus.

The Peloponnesus . . . the Turks . . . malaria . . . death! Terrified, Sophia Dorothea forgot to obey her mother and instead clung to her lover. Greece had already contributed indirectly to her downfall. Two years earlier Königsmark had been laid low by a serious attack of malaria and, panicked, she had run to see him at night. . . .

Sophia Dorothea was at Celle when the expected war against Denmark broke out. The Danes invaded the Duchy of Celle; the ducal domains were looted and the Duke of Celle almost thought of taking refuge abroad. Sophia Dorothea greeted these catastrophes with an indifference which would appear monstrous if she had not been so possessed by her love that nothing else existed for her. She simply wrote to Philipp Christoph with regret that it would be a bad moment to ask her father for the money she needed in order to strike that same father the terrible blow of fleeing from Hanover. For she thought of flight more and more frequently.

And Königsmark, who had long refused to allow his mistress to ruin herself for him and with him, now also dreamt of this madness in his anguish.

At the beginning of the fatal year 1694, the lovers refused to see the danger signals that surrounded them. In vain Podewils preached to him. In vain the Duchess of Celle redoubled her efforts to save her daughter and tried to arrange a rich marriage for Königsmark. Even the faithful Eleonore de Knesebeck, seeing the approaching storm, begged the Princess to allow her to return to her family. But Sophia Dorothea wept and entreated, and the poor Knesebeck gave in. She would pay for it dearly.

Having examined her marriage contract (rather late in the day), Sophia Dorothea realized that she was completely dispossessed and had at her disposal only the small sums given her by the Elector, who was the master of her dowry. So she schemed within her family, first trying to set her mother against George Louis so that her parents should not continue to advise her to live on good terms with her husband. Then she flattered the wily Bernstorff ("I do not entirely trust him," she said naively) so that he would use his influence on the Duke of Celle to obtain for her an "independent establishment." The Duchess of Celle wanted the Parliament of Celle to make Sophia Dorothea a present of 30,000 écus. The Princess was playing a difficult game that was complicated by the Danish invasion of the duchy, by the bombardment and destruction of the fortress of Ratzeburg, which was disputed by Denmark, Sweden, and Hanover, and by the fact that the Duke feared more and more for his own fortune.[10]

Sophia Dorothea would have needed skill, tact, and patience, but these were virtues that she lacked and Königsmark could not give them to her, he who was forever harassing her with reproaches and his insane jealousy. The presence of Prince Maximilian caused tragicomic complications. It was a game of knife, stone, and paper. Königsmark wanted the Princess to leave Celle for Hanover, where he could come to see her incognito. But at Hanover she would have to live in the same palace as her young brother-in-law, Maximilian, of whom Königsmark was jealous. So Königsmark for-

---

[10] It makes one think of Stendhal's letter to Madame X in 1824: "Her husband is a fierce man who loves in his wife only her immense dowry and who would be delighted to dishonor her, relegate her to the country, and alone enjoy her 40,000 pounds of annual income."

bade Sophia Dorothea to go to Hanover, threatening not to see her if she did. On the other hand, he so obviously craved to see her that everyone noticed:

"So it is true that you have forgotten me," Königsmark wrote to his beloved, "and that the pleasures of the theater, music, and, what is worse, foreigners are the cause. I learned all this from the Prince [Electoral Prince] with whom I dined today. . . . As I entered the court in this state everyone looked at me. The Prince himself was good enough to ask me what was wrong, finding me looking so exhausted and wan. I pretended to have had a most painful stomachache."

Königsmark sought to blame someone for his suffering and of course he took his revenge on the victim who offered herself and who loved him too much to defend herself. He wrote that he had never loved before knowing her, and it is easy to believe him. What other woman would have endured what she endured? The jealous man was enraged by everything; the idea that a man should be in her theater box put him in a frenzy. His dream would have been to lock up his mistress in a cage which no male would be allowed to approach. The thought of a man being at all close to her was intolerable to him. He could not even bear the idea of the French ambassador offering the Princess his arm while she descended a staircase!

This almost visceral intolerance, which might possibly have been natural in an Oriental monarch, is hard to believe in a Scandinavian gentleman, familiar with the courts of Europe. He was not even aware how odd the court must have found the distant coldness of the Princess, which his jealousy imposed on her. He did not realize how that behavior attracted attention to her and put her in danger.

"Love is not an honorable sentiment," said Sido, the mother of Colette. This was true for Sophia Dorothea. It is rather frightening to realize how her passion had changed her. She never again had a thought or a word for her children; she hated her parents-in-law, and came close to hating her parents. The world had lost all interest and all color for her. It was a bleak desert containing only the flame that was devouring her. Her only thought was to bury herself in the arms of her lover and not budge again until her death. Without him "four high walls," as she said prophetically, would be her only desire.

That desire would be granted.

Königsmark was the first of the three great lovers from the north who were adored by queens. All three met tragic deaths, and the women they loved also died miserably. There was Königsmark and Sophia Dorothea, then Struensee and Queen Caroline Matilda of Denmark,[11] and finally Fersen and Marie Antoinette.

Deaf to all advice, Königsmark and Sophia Dorothea wrote each other hundreds of letters, each more passionate and more compromising than the last.

---

[11] Matilda, Queen of Denmark and wife of Christian VII, was accused of criminal relations with the king's doctor and favorite, Struensee, who became prime minister. Struensee, an enemy of the nobility and of Russia, was tried and beheaded in 1772. By a strange coincidence, Matilda too is buried in Celle.

5 / Correspondence between Sophia Dorothea and Count von Königsmark

The history of these letters is itself a romance. Without the devotion of a secretary and of a confidante, without the filial piety of a family, we would have nothing with which to support the overdramatized account that contemporaries left of the drama that took place in July 1694. The Hanoverians believed that they had destroyed everything, for they had looked everywhere for letters and other evidence, ransacking Königsmark's and Sophia Dorothea's rooms, seizing the *Journal* later kept by the captive Princess, as well as all other papers found at Ahlden after her death. They carefully burned everything that contained an allusion to the event, even the dispatches of the British envoy to the Hanoverian court. These George Louis had removed from the state archives when he became George I of England. What would he have said if he had learned that the dark and tragic story was safe in a sealed parcel in Sweden? The least of the letters in that parcel would have collapsed the argument so carefully constructed by the lawyers to save the honor of the house of Hanover.

Sophia Dorothea and Philipp Christoph wrote each

other in code, but a code so childishly simple that one wonders how they could have believed that this transparent veil would hide their secret. The names of people and places were replaced either by nicknames or numbers. Thus George Louis was the Reformer; Ernst August was Don Diego; the Duke of Celle, the Grumbler; the Duchess, the Pedagogue; the Electress Sophia, 200; Prince Maximilian, 112; Königsmark, 120; Sophia Dorothea, 201; Herrenhausen, 302; and Celle, 305. Schnath[1] made a complete key to the code. Still more childish was the trick, used by all schoolchildren, of inserting a prearranged group of letters between the syllables of a name. For Sophia Dorothea, for example, the letters were "jill."

The coded surnames spoke for themselves: the Adventuress or the Sultana were enough to make flesh and blood of the famous Aurora of Königsmark; Thyrsis[2] painted Königsmark better than a full-length portrait; the Pedagogue was perfect for the poor Duchess of Celle, whose advice was never followed. With Clumsy Heart we have Sophia Dorothea to the life, her innocent awkwardness and her catastrophic unwillingness to compromise. Madame Platen could walk straight into the pigeonhole labeled The Fat Girl, and Podewils, the obliging and helpful general, was well nicknamed The Good Man.

Königsmark's first letter was written from Ath on July 1, 1690. Extracts have already been quoted from it.

Only one of Königsmark's letters is reproduced here in its original form. It is so badly written that it is touching. We have put the other letters into intelligible French, for we cannot expect the reader to take the trouble

[1] See George Schnath, op. cit. (table at end of the book).
[2] Thyrsis, a shepherd, engaged in a poetical contest with Corydon in Vergil's seventh Eclogue. — Trans.

to decipher the extravagant phonetic spellings that were
even more distorted by the writer's German accent.   Thus
"paquet" (parcel) was written "bake" in the Count's
original French.

For curious readers, here is one of Königsmark's letters
in its original form:

Berlin 23 avril 1691.

*mais Maistresse m'aurais émpesché de sonjer à vous,
aux Dieux est il possible, que vous croje cela, et si je
vous avois poin écris de tous (quo que celci est la 4ᵐᵉ
lettrere) vous devries jamais avoir eus telle penses, ce
postil que vous croje que j'aime quel autre que vous, non
je vous proteste qu'apres vous je n'aimeray jamais plus,
il ne seras pas for difficile de tenir parolle, car appres con
vous à addorer, post on trouver d'autre Famme jolie, vous
vous faite tors, decroire telle schose, et comment pourie
vous faire une comparaison de vous et les autres et se post
il c'apres avoir aimé une Deessé, lon pusse regarder les
Mortels, non énverité je suis de tros bong gous, et je ne
suis poin de ses jang qui voilje s'encanailjser; je vous
addore scharmante brunetté, et je moureray avec ses
sentiment, si vous m'oblije pas, je vous jure que je vous
aimeray toute ma vie je n'atten plus de vos lettres,
parceque, je pretemps d'aistre bientos aupres de vous,
et mon unique occupation allors seras de vous montre,
que je vous aime à la follie, et que rien
m'ay plus schaire que vos grace, adieux, $\dfrac{le\ 3^{me}}{23}$.
je vois que le plaisir que je maitait fais à vous émbras-
ser s'évanuit entieremens puisque l'incomode à paru si
brusquement, je vous avoue que se visaje m'a bien deplus*

*can je lay appersu, un cous de foudre m'auray pas plus
pus surprendre, mais jl faux qui ly aye toujor des faschos
visajes qui empesche, un doux éntretien comme celuy
que nous devien croir, selong tous épparance devray
aître, ouy j'an nay eus l'idé si remplis de joy, que je nay
pus dormir toute la nuit, mais helas tout est vanuis, et
il faux que je passe la seconde nuit sans dormir, et avec
du jagrein aux lieux que la premiere me rejouissay, j lay
sur qu'a moin que vous n'aje la bonté de me consoler, je
me bienjeray dans mes larmes, consolé moy dong divine
bosté, et soulajes un homme, etc.*

*(Translator's note: The following is an attempted transla-
tion of the foregoing letter, which is in places barely
comprehensible.)*

Berlin, April 23, 1691

But Mistress, would you have prevented me from
thinking of you? Oh God, is it possible that you could
think such a thing? If I had not written to you at all
(even though this is the fourth letter) you should never
have had such thoughts. Can it be that you think that I
love someone other than you? No, I swear to you that
after you I will never love again. It will not be very
difficult to keep my word, for after having adored you,
how could one find another pretty woman? You are doing yourself an injustice to think such things, and how
could you make comparisons between yourself and
others? And how could it be that after having loved a
Goddess, one could wish to look upon Mortals? No, in
truth I have too good taste, and I am not one of those who
would like to become a scoundrel. I adore you charming

brunette, and I will die with these feelings, if you do not forget me, I swear to you that I will love you all my life. I expect no letters from you because I hope to be soon near you, and my only occupation will then be to show you that I love you madly, and that nothing is dearer to me than your favours, adieu, $\dfrac{\text{the 3rd}}{23}$

I can see that the pleasure I had imagined in embracing you has completely vanished since the troublesome one appeared so quickly. I must admit to you that his face displeased me greatly when I saw him, and a thunderbolt would not have surprised me more. But it always happens that some unpleasant faces prevent sweet conversations like the one which should have taken place, were we to believe all appearances. Yes my thoughts were so full of joy that I could not sleep the whole night. But alas all this is vanished, and I must spend the second sleepless night in sadness whereas the first night so gladdened me. I am sure that unless you have the goodness to comfort me, I will bathe in my tears. Thus console me, divine beauty, and comfort a man, etc.

The most famous love letters make choice pages in an anthology. They contain the passionate outbursts to which the eloquence of the heart has led the hand and brain. You can feel the warmth of human bodies in them. Such letters are jumbled, confused, contradictory, disorderly; their moral and actual disorganization, their lack of dates, their hidden meanings, their clumsy codes, their outbursts of temper, their repetitions, their illegible scribbles make one feel the breath of the writer, smell the sweat, hear the short panting breaths of a woman afraid of being surprised, and of a man fleeing prying eyes. . . . We are witnesses, partisans, accomplices. We are in the presence of life itself.

What is a love letter if not a certificate of suffering, testimony that the writer has traveled every inch of the road to the cross with its plateaus of jealousy, suspicion, and terror, by a being panic-stricken by the other's absence. Reading such letters we tremble before closed doors on which someone is pounding; centuries later we suffer before the fading image of those features distorted by emotion.

With the passage of time the poignant lines of these letters become dimmer but their intensity does not disappear. Those written in invisible ink suddenly loom up from the white paper under the effect of heat. Once unsealed these letters become desperate appeals despite the falterings of coded writing and the confusion of fictitious names that make them so difficult to decipher at night by the light of a flickering candle. . . . In these letters emotions alternate with everyday details, ducal receptions, fighting, military parades. Passion interrupts the daily round and daily life merges with the eternal.

The letters are sometimes rather long and frequently repetitive, but what cries of love!

" . . . I could never stop loving you and you will make all the unhappiness of my life just as you have made all its happiness. . . ."

" . . . Without you life would be intolerable and four high walls would give me more pleasure than to remain in the world. . . ."

" . . . I have a passion which creates all the pleasure and all the misfortune of my life. It is the only one I can say I have ever felt and it will die with me. . . ."

" . . . If I must renounce seeing you I shall at the same time renounce the whole world. . . ."

" . . . I was born to love you. . . ."

And Königsmark replied, prophetically:

"My lot is that of the butterfly burned by the candle; I cannot avoid my destiny."

Jealousy and fear dominated the relationship between the two lovers. It was a curious kind of jealousy, coming from this man who was adored, handsome, satisfied, and who had nothing for which to reproach his mistress. But there are as many kinds of jealousy as there are men, and the most tenacious are often the least justified.

For her it was fear that cast a terrifying shadow over her love. In the silence of the old castle, with Knesebeck listening for the slightest sound, she would write furtive letters. In the morning they would be entrusted to an officer leaving on a mission, or a postilion believed to be trustworthy, or a well-paid lackey, or a traveler unaware of the bombshell he was carrying in his baggage. . . . Sophia Dorothea's terrors were increased by her solitude within those hostile walls. She took fright as a doe does at the least cracking of a branch. Above all she was anxious about the fate of the absent one, alert to the announcement of each battle, full of nightmares about hand-to-hand combat, and cannonballs carrying off heads. . . . Königsmark's visits only served to redouble the Princess's anguish: His nocturnal visits, the delays, his departures dangerously late at dawn—all her joy could be jeopardized by a spy.

It was such terrible torture that Sophia Dorothea could no longer bear it. It broke her and she let herself drift until she passionately called for the moment when she could flee Hanover.

Königsmark, respectfully in love, writes:

Ath, July 1, 1690

I am now desperate and only a letter from your incomparable hand can save me. If I were fortunate enough to receive one I would be at least somewhat consoled. I hope you will be charitable enough not to refuse me this favor, and because you are the cause of my affliction it is only fair that you should also comfort me. Thus it rests with you to console me for the grief that this sad absence is causing me, and I will see from this whether I can believe the things that you had the kindness to tell me sometimes. If I were not writing to a person for whom I have as much respect as love, I would find better words to express my passion, but as I fear to offend you I must end here and I beg you only to remember me a little bit and to believe that I am your slave.

Hamburg, July 24

I received the answer today. You can imagine how anxious I have been all this time. I can assure you that that is why my illness has lasted so long, because the fear that you had entirely forgotten me caused me severe

---

[1] For the detailed history of the correspondence, see page 253.

pain. Now that I see I was wrong, I have so taken courage that I hope to see you before long.

Furthermore, if one can believe these words, I shall never change unless you compel me to. How happy I would be; my bliss would then be perfect and I would wish for none other in the world. But these words mean a great deal and I do not know whether you have reflected. If you would do me the favor of replying two words I would get well much sooner.

April (or May 20) 1691

Never was a mortal more joyful than I when I received your letter on arriving here. I flatter myself that I am now in your good graces, and at the same time I am losing all the weak suspicions which had troubled my heart. . . . My noble companion [Prince Ernst] will be able to tell you of the state he finds me in daily. As you may imagine, I am hiding my reasons from him. Perhaps you won't believe him but, on the word of an honorable man, I have a number of times been so beside myself that I thought I would faint, and yesterday evening, while I was out walking, thinking of how many days I must spend without seeing you, I was so upset that I had a palpitation of the heart, and I was obliged to return home. Had not my servant brought me a cordial I do not know what would have happened to me. It took me a long time to recover, and without your very dear letter, I would have gone to pieces altogether. Adieu, amiable brunette, I embrace your knees.

. . . If you felt guilty, you would not have done me the kindness of writing to me, but after all that you have done to me, I still must adore you. However, your contemptuous behavior has made me decide to leave tomorrow. If you still wish to comfort a poor heart torn by jealousy tell me to come you know where. As that is perhaps the only favor I shall ask of you, because I hope that the good Lord will rather take me from this world rather than let me suffer in this way, I implore you not to refuse it. But although you may force me to make other decisions, I shall never cease loving you.

The Princess doubtless granted him this favor, for Philipp Christoph's tone rapidly changed from that of a bashful lover to a reassured and already demanding lover. What enraged him above all was the reserve with which she was obliged to treat him in public.

. . . Alas! I love my own destruction,
And nurse a fire within my breast
Which will soon consume me.
I am well aware of my own perdition,
Because I have dared to love
What I should only have worshiped.

Und also lieb ich mein Verderben
Und häge ein feuer in meiner brust
daran ich doch zulest musst sterben
Mein Untergant ist mir gar wil bewust
Das magst ich habe lieben wollen
Was ich viel mehr anbâten sollen

To satisfy Königsmark, the Princess drew up a detailed daily account of her life and sent it every day to her lover. She dared refuse him nothing and did not even reflect on the dangers these accounts exposed her to, for a single one of them would have been sufficient to identify her.

. . . If you wish to oblige me let me know with whom you talked at court. It is not out of jealousy that I wish to know, but out of curiosity. If you are kind enough to reply, the same messenger will receive your answer at the same places. If by chance you should be playing in the great hall, my man will wait in the gallery leading to your apartments so as not to be seen. You have laid down a law which I shall find hard to keep, but since you wish it, I must obey. I hope, however, that you will give me permission to come and see you in your apartments this evening. If you don't agree to that, come and visit me tonight at my house. Let me know one way or the other. If you decide to come to me you will find that everyone in my household has retired. The door will be open. Come in boldly without being afraid of anything. I am dying with impatience to see you. Answer quickly so that I may know what to expect.

Adieu, dear heart, *ricorda li cor mio.* . . .

It is true that I am not too satisfied with the coldness you showed me yesterday. It is the reason why I passed a most miserable night. I was so sad I could not stop myself from crying, and all these emotions gave me a fever for nearly three hours. I assure you my divine beauty that for as long as I can remember I have not been in such a state. I said to myself: "the good Lord is punishing me with sickness, but that is not enough; at the same time He has frozen the heart of my goddess. This is intolerable, and I can't stand it." I threw myself on my knees, tears in my eyes, and prayed to the good

Lord that He bring me death if it were true that you loved me no longer.

April 12, 1691

I am shut up here in my room and see no one. I never budge and my thoughts take me away from everything. You are my only preoccupation. If by chance an officer wishes to speak to me about the regiment I am furious at losing so much time not thinking of you. . . . Yet I must confess to you that I have made a choice here, not of a pretty girl but of a bear which I have in my room and which I feed so that if you should fail to keep faith with me, I will give him my breast and let him tear my heart out. I am teaching him this trick with sheep and calves. He is learning quite well and if, God forbid, I ever need to have him perform it on me, I shall not suffer long.

Adieu. Think of me.

February 24, 1692

You say that you see no one, which is the most obliging thing in the world. But you see the Reformer [George Louis] all the more, which makes me fear that you will little by little become accustomed to his mediocre caresses and that he will kiss you so often that I die of grief simply to think of it. For your own self respect don't become accustomed to it. Always think of the way he treats you—you who are worthy of all honest, obliging, and respectful behavior. But I am seeing the faults of another, and I cannot help thinking that the Reformer did not always behave in this way, and I am the most criminal. What you have told me yourself is so unkind that

I die only to think of it. I am unfortunate to love you so tenderly, and this extraordinary passion makes me so hateful. Please think no longer of the past, I beg of you. Adieu, alas adieu.

. . . I saw your windows open (the Reformer was coming out of your dressing room) without seeing you. Although I spoke quite loudly and walked back and forth, I didn't see a living soul. As it was late I think you were already with the Roman lady [the Electress]. I would be inconsolable if I did not have the hope of seeing you this evening at six. What a state I am reduced to: I count it the greatest happiness in the world to see you a thousand feet away.

July 23 (August 2) from the camp
. . . As I may perhaps be ordered to march to Lunen, let me know if I can't come by Celle without offending anyone. If you are not there, it is required by protocol. . . . I may be mistaken, but on rereading the eleventh letter I did not find it as tender nor as sincere as the tenth. Let me know if I am mistaken. . . . Perhaps you think I am not loving because I don't ask you to come, but think of what prevents me from doing so. However if you really desire it, I would beg you to come. But I would be perhaps two days here and then your neighbor [Max] would have the field to himself. He has loved you even if he has been indifferent to you. I am still afraid of him although there is scarcely anything to fear. But the fact that he has been on quite familiar terms with you is reason enough to fear his impertinence. Indeed, it would be vexing to see a man close to you who could see you through twenty little holes, besides the fact

that you could not say a word out of his hearing. . . . I know the power of a mother whom one loves, and when she gives you the chance you must be wise enough to be able to resist. My blood boils when I think that your mother, to revenge herself on the Electoral Prince, might have you made a cuckold of him, and whenever I think that you might ever caress anyone but me, my blood curdles in my veins. . . . Oh God, if I ever saw you kiss anyone with as much passion as you have kissed me, and ride astride with the same desire, I never want to see God if it would not drive me mad. Even writing to you about it my hand trembles and I have difficulty going on, so let us change the subject. . . . From the attached letter you will see how once again efforts are being made to persuade me to marry the daughter of Monsieur Bielke,[2] but my answer was that I would rather starve than do so and that I begged him to speak no more to me of marriage for it might cause a falling out between us. . . . If you want to wait until Prince Max is bored, I won't see you for a long time, because when he is with the Electress and his thin divinity he is as happy as a king. I would not have believed that this ape could have given me as much worry as he does, and I wish he were at the farthest end of Hungary where he would not give me such heartache as he does now. One could not speak more obligingly about starving than you do, and although it would be a great consolation to me to see you always at my side, but do you think that I would wish to lead you into poverty? No, no, don't believe it. You must live happy and contented while waiting for me to seek a glorious death to cut short my unhappy days, and die as the Electoral Princess's lover. . . . I would never

---

[2] The Swedish Field Marshal Niels Bielke.

accept the idea that your passion is greater than mine, and I would be inconsolable if I hadn't given you the basic proofs of this, for you might think that vanity would attach me to you, as you are a Princess. No, I swear to you, if you were the daughter of the executioner I would love you with just as much ardor.

Although I had resolved to write you tomorrow and simply to reply to your letters no. 13, 14, and 15 which I received at the same time, I shall be deprived of this pleasure because the King [Willem of Orange] has decided to attack the French army tomorrow, which is two hours away. The place is called Enghien. At any other time this news would have filled me with joy. . . . I have risked my life a hundred times by stupidity or lightheartedness, and I know myself well enough to realize that death has never frightened me. But, my goddess, what makes me a coward is the fear of never seeing you again. . . . However, don't believe that you have a cowardly suitor. No, my dear, since I must fight I shall behave as I must and I hope to distinguish myself. But, my heart, allow me to make you a prayer which is that if my destiny wishes me enough ill to deprive me of an arm or a leg, do not forget me, and have a little kindness for a wretch whose sole pleasure has been to love you . . . a man who has been truly attached to you and who will continue to be for the rest of his life, crippled though he may be. My eyes, which have been charmed by yours, may not see them again. I cannot think about that without crying. Oh, how little I take advantage of being loved by you, and how much torment you cause me. The church bells of Halle are striking twelve. Cannonballs, powder, and fuses are being brought in. It is the prologue for the scene which we must act out tomorrow and

I must go and do my duty. Adieu, beloved child. Ah, I am greatly to be pitied. From the camp at Halle, the 23rd.

To which the Princess replied:

I am charmed by everything you tell me. Rest assured that whatever accident might befall you, you would not be loved the less. My affection is equal to any test, and even if only your head were left, I would always love you to distraction, and would count it a real pleasure to renounce the world in order to live with you wherever you please. However, I am very happy that you came back in one piece. Every bit of you is so handsome and so charming that none of it must be lost. Look after yourself, I beg you.

The jealous Königsmark answered:

And to crown it all, I had to listen to it said that my close friend and his troublesome companion had the pleasure of talking to you. . . . Since this incident I have been imagining strange things and I am stupid enough to believe that yesterday's incident forebodes my misfortune, and that it is the same man who has caused all this grief. . . . I will have him watched closely and if I hear the least thing believe my word as a gentleman that I will never see you again and that I would rather explore the length and breadth of Lapland than appear again before those eyes which have charmed me. . . . Without that I would have had the pleasure of serving you, instead of seeing this joy in the hands of a man whom I loathe and who is sufficiently impertinent to come and tell me about it himself, telling me of the state you were in, your undress, uncoifed, your hair hanging down loose on your matchless bosom. Oh God, I cannot write for anger!

The joy of seeing the Reformer leave was cut short by the sadness of seeing you ill. . . . I hope to kiss you tomorrow evening. I await the usual signal, and the bad weather will not prevent me from enjoying the pleasure of your delightful embraces.

Instructions from the Princess:

. . . Let him wait at 8 o'clock in the evening by the door of the great hall where the Princess usually plays. He can see her from there in complete safety, for no one will pass by, tomorrow being Sunday.

Königsmark's answer:

He will be there at the appointed hour. Do not doubt his faithfulness.

From the camp, near Wavre
. . . What saddens me most is that when you see me next you will find me as ugly as anything. The Elector has told me so, and all my friends find me so downhearted that they have difficulty recognizing me. Every day people ask if I am sick, but my sickness comes only from loving, my cruel little one. I hope you will be pleased with me, as I am with you, and now that it is all over I can tell you that all the jealous suspicions I had of you put me into such a state that my servants were sorry for me and believed that I had colic. I assure you that if

your feelings for me had changed, I would have died of grief. . . .

. . . When I have what I am seeking, I shall hope to see you, to hold you in my arms. . . . I must tell you about the nasty thing that the Duke of Richmond tried to do. He was at a debauch with Duke Fredric [sic][3] and some girls. The party went so far that after they had debauched themselves in all sorts of ways, the Duke of R. wanted to force the girls to be served by a large German mastiff, if you see what I mean! This is taking fun a bit far. . . . The Duke of Saxony has promised me to come to Hanover for carnival. . . .

. . . I dined at Celle. Their Highnesses asked if the Princess was still in Hanover. I told them that I had had the honor of playing with her and with the Electress on Saturday, and that I had not seen her since. Madame de Buleau gave me so much to drink that I was completely drunk. They took me to Madame de Boidavis', but I do not remember what I did or said.

Sophia Dorothea often visited her parents at Brockhausen and in Celle. For his part, Königsmark accompanied the Elector, with whom he was still in favor, to Brunswick, but these separations were short and Königsmark managed to make them shorter still by going secretly to Celle. The Duchess of Celle was, of course, unaware of these visits.

. . . What I wouldn't give to hear midnight strike! Be

---

[3] Frederick of Saxony. — Trans.

sure to have smelling salts ready lest my excess of joy cause me to faint. Tonight I shall embrace the most agreeable person in the world and I shall kiss her charming lips. . . . I shall hear you tell me yourself that I matter to you in some way. I shall embrace your knees; my tears will be allowed to run down your incomparable cheeks; my arms will have the satisfaction of embracing the most beautiful body in the world. . . .

Königsmark was at bay. His enormous gambling debts prevented him from returning to distinguish himself on the Flanders front, where his creditors awaited him. His estates in Sweden were about to be confiscated on the King's orders. He could not accept the advantageous offers made to him because they would oblige him to leave Hanover and Sophia Dorothea whom he had vowed never to leave. When he wrote that he had sacrificed everything for her, he was not lying. At this point she had only sacrificed her repose for him.

Their correspondence had become nothing more than an unduly long lament. The Princess's letters are saved from monotony by their passion; those of Königsmark by their gaiety. In spite of everything he laughed—in recounting to his beloved the minor incidents of camp life, the story of the old red ribbon, of the lover who was too good an accountant, of the strange debauch of the handsome Duke of Richmond, Charles II's bastard by the beautiful Louise de Kéroualle. He could laugh when painting the portrait of August the Strong, the future Elector of Saxony, or when devising a thousand preposterous ways of seeing his Princess again, such as disguising himself as a beggar and demanding alms at the gates of the palace where Sophia Dorothea would have to take off her glove to give him a pittance.

Dist, November 6

... I have written a song in German about my lovely one, and when I sang it at a party, many people asked me about it. I told them that the beauty was called Léonisse and they all entreated me to start toasting that name and the song too. This put me in a good mood and I got drunk with them. To make the wine more pleasant, I found an old, very dirty red ribbon among my things and I made them swallow it. You know from whom this ribbon comes. This is the only day I have been a little happy for three weeks. . . .

August 15

... I told you that I was drunk. Don't for a moment believe that I am capable of being unfaithful to you. No, my angel, I have never once thought of that. By this you can see that I will not get drunk just to have a pretext for misbehaving. . . .

... If I were the Lord of Creation I would throw her [Countess Platen] to the bears to be eaten. The lions would drink her diabolical blood; the tigers would tear out her cowardly heart. I would spend night and day seeking out new torments for her. . . .

... For six days we have been only four leagues from Brussels, and I haven't once thought of setting foot in the town. Yesterday there was a great feast which they call here the Feast of the Miracles, and all the important people and the generals, and many beautiful ladies went to it in post chaises. My soldiers went too, but I swear my Léonisse that I did not even think of going. . . . The Duke of Portland has been very friendly and has assured me that the King [William III of England] held me in esteem, but I don't even think of bettering my fortune in that way. . . . The King's talk with our Prince was very dull for both are men of few words. . . . Yesterday our Prince went to see His Majesty in his camp. I was not in his suite, but tomorrow I shall accompany the Prince when he goes to visit the Elector. . . . Prince Frederick August of Saxony is everyone's dupe, for they cheat him when it comes to his horses, and they take his money at cards. He has already lost a thousand pistoles. No one advises him and he is ruining himself.

. . . Yesterday I went to the grand army. We paid our respects to the Elector of Bavaria, then joined the King, who was walking in the camp. There was a great gathering of people of quality but no very distinguished-looking men. The good Elector was most gracious to me and his behavior was full of kindness and courtesy. The [Electoral] Prince is very worried about his troops; it is obvious that he is scarcely able to command them.

I swear to you that what Duke Frederick [of Saxony] told me about the Marionette [the Duchess of Saxony-Eisenach] has not affected me because she disgusted me even before I heard it. Her behavior reveals the sort of woman she is. . . . I have not said even a word about you to him [to Duke Frederick]. He has cut himself with his saber, making a large wound in his head, whereas he wanted to cut off Monteney's head. I visit him every day. He is most uncomfortable and dirty in his bed. With all those bandages around his head and that terrible mouth of his he is not a pleasant sight. But he is a good sort of prince. I wish that he would become elector [of Saxony], for he would see to it that I got some good breaks.

You have heard about Ferdinand's affair [a courtier,

the lover of the Electress of Brandenburg, who was the daughter of Princess Sophia]. Not only did he lose all his money, he owes 2,000 pistoles besides. The Huguenots who won the money from him have not been paid and have complained to the Prince of Anhalt. The Prince commanded the illustrious lover to pay his debts before leaving Berlin. Ferdinand, in a rage, went to the Electress, who was so peeved by the affront to her favorite that she sent word to the Prince of Anhalt that she was astounded at the liberty he had taken and that she would complain to the Elector. The Prince humbly begged pardon, but the funniest part of the story is yet to come: The Electress decided to take Ferdinand with her to Luisburg, but he has an acknowledged mistress who begged that she be allowed to keep her Ferdinand, and said that she would pay his debts. The Electress screamed that she was taking Ferdinand along for her own pleasure, and that when she had had enough of him, she would send him back to the other one. There's a happy man.

Deinze, September 3, new style
. . . I have just returned from a walk with the King. The Duke of Richmond was there, but he was as drunk as a lord, and doing all sorts of silly things. . . .

My pet, you must decide my fate and it is on you that my happiness depends. You are my goddess.

Deinze, September 6/16, 92
. . . The Duke of Richmond amuses himself by getting drunk and inventing new oaths. The other day I dined with him at Count Egmond's. He had invented an abominable new curse which is: "God's belly, stuffed

with apostles." That's how our youth enjoy themselves. I am their tutor and scold them well.

The Ball [the hereditary Princess of Prussia] has been very much at odds with Montalban. She made fun of him because people say his legs were getting too fat.

The next day he visited the Electress in her room and she teased him about the same thing. He lost his temper, put his leg up on her dressing table, and said: "All the people who have told you those things have lied."

Poor Croseck, seeing that Montalban had been too impertinent, came up to him with the intention of making him withdraw, but contrary to her expectation she received such a slap that she began to bleed at the mouth and eyes. The Electress flew into a rage and forbid Montalban ever to see her again and [ordered him] to leave the house. But she did not hold to that resolution for long because some of his friends interceded for him and he and the Electress made it up again. . . .

There was a great debauch at Ovenair's the evening before last: the Elector, the Prince, Busch, Count Schlitenbach, Königsmark and a man called Simony were there with five whores, two of them very pretty. But I behaved myself because I only ate and drank. The Elector is one of the most agreeable men I have seen for a long time at this sort of debauch, and he made such fun of these wretched trollops that he made them cry. They did not know who he was and showered him with curses. This went on until 2 o'clock. He is in pretty bad shape.

5/15

The lieutenant who went to the court brought me a large packet [of letters] and I was overjoyed thinking surely that there would be some from you. But I was very much mistaken because I found only letters from Prince Ernst and from the Field Marshal. Everyone writes but you. I have said so much that I will say nothing more. You danced at Colt's ball. . . .

1692—It was a year of war between the Allies and Louis XIV, with interminable sieges, endless marches and counter-marches, and eternal winter bivouacs, exasperating the lovers which they separated. Königsmark asked again and again for sick leave as a pretext to rush to Hanover, but the court of Hanover, which was not blind, had its reasons for keeping the burdensome "Chevalier" away, and while leaves of absence were granted all around him, they were pitilessly refused to him. Finally, he could stand it no longer. One night he galloped up to the old castle, bathed in sweat and covered with mud. He did not even take the time to change his clothes at his house, so great was his haste to see his "Léonisse" again. He had been on horseback for six days and nights and he would have ridden over anyone, even the Elector, who would have tried to stop him. The leave that had been refused him he took on his own authority, pretending to be sick and slipping off in secret. If he had been discovered, he would have been considered a deserter. But Philipp Christoph was careless and reckless, counting on his luck. Luck, this time, was called the Marshal Podewils, The Good Man. He saved Königsmark by granting him formal leave and, better still, with the order to remain in Hanover. It was marvelous!

The Duchess of Celle, realizing the danger Königsmark represented for her daughter, and knowing that he was financially ruined and in ill favor at court, tried to marry him off to a rich heiress and get Sophia Dorothea out of the way.

. . . The confidante will tell you that I am more pleased with you since yesterday although I only had the pleasure of squeezing your hands. Our constraint has its charm and I have had some most happy moments during the last seven days when I have seen you in places where the language of the eyes is scarcely allowed. What a delight, my dear child, to tell each other with impunity in the presence of thousands that we love each other! . . .

I have had a long conversation with the Duchess of Celle, and I believe her to be the most deceitful woman in the world. She says a thousand nice things and yet she is using her authority to try to ruin me with you. . . .

Königsmark made a terrible, unspecified blunder, for which he humbly asked forgiveness:

. . . If you could see my despair you would pardon me the fault I have just committed. I admit I was irritated at you because you did not deign to look at me during the play, although I was sitting directly opposite you. But I don't deserve this, and my sacrificing the Duchess of Eisenach for you is worth at least a glance. You see that I hardly look at her and when she speaks to me I answer her very briefly so as not to encourage conversation. Her chambermaid has told me that the Duchess finds me changed, and a thousand other things. But a truce to all that; it's not worth talking about. Pardon, Princess, I beg you, and arrange it so that I can see you tomorrow.

. . . I slept like a king and I hope very much you did the same. What joy, what pleasure, what enchantment have I not felt in your arms. God! What a night I have spent. It has made me forget all my grief. . . .

. . . 202 [Countess Platen], when we paid court to her yesterday, proposed a dinner party at an inn where each man would have his "came" [*dame?* for woman]. 120 [I] said promptly: "I shall take the 'Cupsteine' [?] woman." 202 turned scarlet and shouted: "I shall take M. de B'lati [Balatin]." She was in such a bad mood throughout dinner that many people noticed it. I doubt if she will forgive 120 [me] for this offense. . . . Come and comfort my grief.

February 19/29 1692

. . . When I left you I found the company very lively at the Countess's, everyone glass in hand and the music of trumpets and kettledrums, but it all diverted me so little that I wished myself twenty leagues away. My grief was so apparent that Monsieur B. asked me what was wrong because I did not want to pledge him even a glass of wine and didn't. . . . The noise of glasses, trumpets, and kettledrums mingled with the soft sound of flutes and the hoarse cries of the drunks made the funniest harmony in the world and gave me the chance to find a corner where I could daydream in comfort while the others danced, undressed, and jumped up on the table. . . .

. . . Until now I haven't feared that you have forgotten me, but since the arrival of the Piedmontese Count and the one from Ostrige [Austria] I can no longer doubt your inconstancy. Cruel and barbarous woman, is this the reason you imprison hearts? You are dealing with a man who has loved you to distraction; you made me believe you loved me as much. I have gladly neglected fortune and happiness for you, and you treat me like this. It's incredible! But do not believe that I will leave things as they are. No, no, my heart is too proud to be treated as a dupe. I shall avenge myself or die. Yes, I shall avenge myself in a way the whole world will see. . . .

You wanted to stay in your room crying at my departure! Your room was the opera house; your tears came from too much laughing and your consolation, instead of the reading from my letters, has been to hear sweet things from others! It is too much. I cannot think about it any more.

. . . [You consider] the passion you have for me a crime since you believe that God is punishing you for it. Good heavens, what a thought! Don't even imagine such things because I fear that that kind of thought could turn you away from me. You know what our love is based on: Our wishes are according to divine law.

. . . Thursday at 2:00 in the morning.

Your behavior is scarcely kind. You make an appointment and then leave people to freeze to death waiting for the signal. You should know that I was waiting in the streets from 11:30 to 1:00. I don't know what to believe, but I can hardly doubt your inconsistancy any more having suffered so much from it. You did not condescend to look at me all evening. Didn't you purposely avoid playing with me? You want to be rid of me: I shall be the first to leave you. Farewell, then. I am leaving tomorrow for Hamburg.

Having passed the whole night without sleeping I have had the time to think a lot, and this has led me to despair. But I also remembered that I had sworn that I would never leave you abruptly. Moreover, before I go away

I still want to know your reasons; that is why I am still here today.

5/15 July

. . . You tell me in yours: "Let us love each other forever." Did you reflect on what you were writing? It was at the time I believe that your mind was full of thoughts of pleasing the Imperial cavalry captain. Apparently he did not fail to tell you that he had come from the depths of Turkey to admire your beauty. However, he only came to pick up a few hundred ducats with which to refurbish his equipment that was ruined at Grossnardein. . . .

Will Königsmark become a hero like those in L'Astrée?[4] *It would not suit him:*

. . . How hard it is for my heart to stay with me. It keeps trying to leave me and go and thank you for capturing it. . . . I fear I will lose it altogether and that it will no longer want to resume its usual place because you are treating it too affectionately. But I cannot live without a heart, so please, for pity's sake, give me yours. Without the one or the other I cannot live!

Philipp Christoph's letters are cries of passion shot through with affectations in the style of the time, and with bad poetry borrowed from fashionable novels.

4 leagues from Venlo

. . . I am sighing and trembling as I write you this. I have no idea how I stand with you, having received only one of your letters.

---

[4] L'Astrée, an early seventeenth-century pastoral novel by Honoré d'Urfé, celebrated the love of Céladon for Astrée. — Trans.

When I think of past pleasures my misfortunes seem greater to me. I think: "What! You won't kiss those piercing eyes, that divine mouth, that matchless bosom again?" I will never again find myself in those arms which embraced me with pleasure. I shall lose all that by losing you!

December, 1692

... Electoral Princess! Now one can call you that because apparently the Electoral Prince invested you with that title of honor last night. Are embraces more delightful when one has this rank? ... I cannot sleep for rage that an Electoral Prince is depriving me of the pleasure of my charming mistress.

Königsmark arrived secretly in Brockhausen and hid in a neighboring house. As he waited for the princess's signal he made himself as handsome as possible:

I am shaved [he wrote her]. I look fine, and one could sing "The knight is a conqueror." We will recognize each other by the usual signal, I shall whistle "The Spanish Follies" from a distance.

(June) 20

... This is just to let you know that my expedition ended without my meeting anyone, except that on coming out of the gate I saw two men walking about six paces away. I didn't dare turn my head, which prevented me from seeing who they were. One of your maids lit a candle outside the dressing room as I passed through the room, but I don't know which maid it was since I did not dare turn my head. There, my dear heart, are all the incidents that occurred.

Altenburg, September 19, 1693
. . . I do not mind if you are pale, thin, and drawn. I would be most unhappy if my passion were limited only to your beauty. In twenty-four hours it could change to ugliness and then where would I be?

My passion is founded on more solid enchantments in which I shall never see a change. If you were eighty, the beauties of merit last for eternity.

I can swear to you again that I don't remember when my love ever before made me uneasy for even a quarter of an hour. At present, by contrast, there is scarcely a night that I do not sit up half the time. . . . As soon as I met you I gave myself entirely to you. Though reason told me that I would have to leave one day, I did not listen and my heart told me that it would not consent.

My lot will be that of the butterfly who burns in the candle flame. I can not avoid my destiny.

You want to know whether I still want to leave the army. I answer that that depends entirely on you, because as I have resolved to be completely yours, heart, body, and soul, you must rule on how I should conduct myself.

Tuesday, June 21/July 1
. . . The attached letter will show you my estate in Sweden, which is rather poor. But I have acquired a much greater treasure and I defy this barbaric king to take it away from me. I have your very dear person and the possession of your heart. If I did not have you to

console me, Léonisse, I would die of despair. But at present I live peacefully and with resolution.

I think we will be marching toward the end of the month. They are giving me a detachment of a thousand infantrymen, and I command this little unit. I don't know if I should regard this as a favor. . . .

There is a nice story about the young daughter of a Brussels merchant and a Dutch lieutenant who was garrisoned there this winter. .ˆ. . The lieutenant courted the girl and got into such good favor with her that they made an agreement, signed with their blood, according to which the lieutenant agreed to give her 5 rixdalers for each visit on which he kissed her. The girl in turn promised the lieutenant 10 rixdalers for each time she asked him to come or gave him a date. The poor father, who is very rich, was the victim of the contract, because the young man managed matters so well that in the course of his winter quarters he won 6,000 rixdalers which the girl little by little stole from her father.

The father complained to the generals, who ordered a council of war at which they found that it was money properly acquired. They advised the father to give 2,000 rixdalers to his daughter and that the lieutenant would marry her. This the father did because the girl was pregnant.

. . . Relieve me quickly of my suspicion and do not allow it to take root in this odd and jealous frame of mind with which I regard the world.

Farewell, beloved little one.

June 30/July 10, Friday at noon
. . . The life I have been leading since the court returned should cause you much jealousy for I play each night

with ladies who, without vanity, are neither ugly nor of base rank. I ask your pardon, but I could not live without this pleasure. As one of the ladies resembles you, I cannot help being in her company. You will be curious to know who it is, but I will not tell you for fear that you might forbid me to pay her court. I would be inconsolable.

Sunday (June 2/July 12)
. . . You ask me not to go with the army. I will obey you blindly and without second thoughts on the condition that if, to save my honor, I were obliged to go, you would give me permission. . . .

Madame,
    What will you say, Madame, when you learn that they did not let me go through the day without inflicting the misfortune I have so much feared. Monsieur Podewils was the first to warn me to be careful of my behavior. . . .
    . . . The Innocent[5] warned me of the same thing, and as he was not as cautious as the other, he admitted that the conversations I have had from time to time with you might have unpleasant consequences for me. I could not stay any longer in the antechamber for fear of a fainting fit after hearing such news.

Sunday (July 2/12)
. . . I received your letter after mine had gone, but I was very upset when I read that your mother has had such a violent quarrel with your father. In the end it is easy

---

[5] Prince Ernst August (sometimes Don Diego).

to see that our side is the weaker one and that we have nothing more to hope for. You will be obliged to tie yourself more closely than ever to the Prince, and I to find some corner of the world where someone will give me enough to eat so that I do not die of hunger. I admit frankly that your father's conduct surprises me, and there is no doubt that it comes by way of the Platen woman who rules Bernstorff absolutely, and the latter is all-powerful with your father. Your previous [letter] gave me much joy because it appeared that Bernstorff wanted to get involved in your behalf, but he is as false as the devil. . . . In the century in which we live, people are not taken in so easily.

October 1

. . . At 2 o'clock I learned the fatal news that the Prince is in your arms. His arrival made me despair. I am beside myself and only death can deliver me from the torments which his presence makes me suffer.

. . . Let me see by your behavior that you are in despair at the unfortunate return of the Prince, and above all let me see that the embraces of the newcomer are killing you.

I am writing to ask Marshal Podewils for a three-day leave. I will be at Zelle [Celle] before you leave. . . . I shall arrive in disguise. Wait for me in the little staircase for two nights until 11 o'clock. I know the way to the hidden staircase and I shall await the signal. . . .

Wednesday, at four in the evening

. . . My constancy is proof against all the world's beauties. The Countess de Lippe, who is young, beautiful, and who is in favor at court, has not succeeded in tempting me at all and up to now I have not set foot in her house. I must do so for civility's sake, however, but I really wanted to give you this evidence of my passion.

. . . I saw you arrive here yesterday. How happy I was! I was at the Field Marshal's when I heard the drum.[6]

(July 17/27)
It is certain that if Prince Max were not so close to you I would much prefer that you were here than with your mad mother, because at least you would not be able to say as an excuse: "She was the one who brought them into my bedroom." It seems to me that you are enjoying yourself, going every day to the theater. But I do not begrudge it. On the contrary, I am glad that you are enjoying yourself, and provided that no one comes into your box or approaches you to whisper sweet nothings in your ear, I am delighted that you should be having fun. I shall try to do the same. . . .

I know very well that there is a door in the apartment in question, but isn't it enough that a person have evil intentions, and what about the secret stairway? But I swear to you that if there were thirty I would not mind. What I have said to you about it is only to find an excuse so that Prince Max should not listen to every word you say or through some crack see you in your nightgown or stark naked about to put one on.

Saturday (July 24/August 3)
. . . I am much obliged to Monsieur Stubenhol for the fine report he made about that supper. Until now his lies have not worried me, but at present I see what many

---

[6] When the Electoral Princess passed, a salute was sounded.

people have told me about him. You know this man and
you know only too well that he makes a little fart into
a thunderclap. It is not surprising that he found my
supper a fine one: He alone ate six partridges and drank
a whole bottle of sherry. For him it was the finest and
grandest banquet in the world. Give him the same thing
in a pig sty and he will see it as the finest Italian flower
garden.

I am going to bed, as it is already two o'clock in the
morning. If I went on I would write things I would be
sorry to say to a lady.

Hanover, (July) 23
. . . I hope that what I dreamt last night will not happen,
for I had my head cut off because I was surprised with
you . . . and I have suffered more than a soul in purga-
tory. My greatest worry was what had become of you.
My judges were the Prince and the Good Man [Marshal
Podewils]. I wouldn't want to spend another such night
for anything in the world. On waking up I was bathed in
sweat and my valet told me that I had shouted with a
sobbing voice: "Where is she, where is she?" I did not
fear death, but my greatest suffering was being deprived
of news of you and not being able any longer to find out
what had become of you. This sort of thing makes one
realize how much one loves people. . . .

. . . The Good Man has returned from the conference and
sent me back the regimental Dragoons without orders.
This is why I think that we will remain this week. As
I shall dine with him tomorrow, I will find out more and
will let you know immediately. Meanwhile, be ready
to do what you will find attached. The Electress has

been to Lindau to take Countess Platen for a walk. . . . Count Stembock, whom you saw here seven years ago, and also the Count of Gardie, wanted to pay their respects. I took them there and found the Fat One [Countess Platen] so heated up that the make-up was running off her face. She was so put off to see so many outsiders arrive that she hardly knew what to do. She chose the best course by retiring immediately to put herself in order again. There is plenty of malice in the Electress, and she could not have a better revenge.

August 1693

. . . Altenburg, the thirteenth. . . . On the twelfth I did what I have done every day, which is to say, drink, eat, and visit the men on duty. The thirteenth I did the same. The Duke of Celle came to visit us . . . Nothing could be more innocent. God willing, I will be able to show you by my conduct that all my thoughts, all my steps, are only for you. . . . I have received the third letter . . . eight days after the one marked four. I don't understand the cause of this delay, but I know that it is dangerous for a letter to be longer on the way.

. . . Tdolo mio, when will I have the joy of holding you in my arms? It's enough to make a Cato despair to think that you could come if Prince Max did not prevent it. . . . But the desire to see you is putting a stop to my jealousy and I beg you to come. How long could I be with you? Perhaps only two days before I will see you among people who hate us and others who want to insinuate themselves into our circle. Do not believe, my angel, that my jealousy comes from the bad opinion that I have of you. That would be too criminal. Rather it comes from

the violence of my passion, and so I flatter myself that you will always excuse me when this madness comes over me.

Sunday

... Go, cruel one, and take your pleasure with your beloved new bedfellow.... You are not content with taking away my peace of mind. You have also robbed me of honor, reputation, and everything that I have in the world. Haven't I neglected everything for you? What is the state of my affairs? You know. I have neglected everything for a kiss, and this is my marvelous reward....

... The continual gatherings at which I shine are assemblies of my dragoons, because I am with them every day, drilling them, and for the past three days I have not been to see anyone on account of the hunt.... I was aware that something was holding you up, but I did not know that it was a very well-built and most magnificent young man. You want me to tell you positively what you ought to do. What the devil do you want me to tell you? If I wanted to please you I would tell you to stay; to taste the pleasures that a new lover produces. If I begged you to come, you would find still another excuse to quarrel with me so that you could stay.

September 1, 1693

... Why do you flatter me so much in your letters when you think so little of keeping your promises to me? You assure me that nothing will be difficult for you and that you will do everything to please me. That's a nice promise, but badly kept. Alas, you tell me: "Let us hope that time may make us happy." But you must know that time makes me the unhappiest of men. . . . I believe they will force me to leave you. I cannot finish this letter for grief, sadness, and anger. Farewell. At least do not hate me because I swear by God I do not merit it at all.

I feel thirsty and feverish. . . . I shall bleed myself so that I don't fall sick. . . . It appears that Monsieur de Sporgue will die, perhaps today. I have 3 captains, 5 lieutenants, and 4 sublieutenants on the verge of death. More than 300 infantrymen and dragoons from our contigent alone are exhausted. The air is noxious and the healthiest are falling ill. All the same, I expect I won't succumb, knowing that you are out of danger. . . . The siege of Charleroi will ensure that the Electoral Prince won't come here immediately. Good God, let this siege deliver us from these tiresome people! They say for certain that things are getting better, but the orders they give for looking after the sick make me tremble with fear that we will not leave this post soon. I am sorry that you have grown so thin, but (with your permission) I find the question you put to me ridiculous and absurd. . . . If I only loved your beauty I would pardon you, but it is not only that I adore, it is your merits. . . . I assure you that were you as ugly as Madame Kopfstein I would not love a whit the less. . . . Do you believe that a passion like mine is based on so transitory a thing as beauty? Although you are more beautiful than any of your sex, I can tell you that it is not that that has put me in my present state. It is true that your beauty has inflamed me, and without it I would perhaps not be as happy as I am, but what has made me what I am is your character, your sincerity, your way of living, and finally, your soul, so well borne and so fair. . . . Truly, Léonisse, your questions cause me much grief. You feared that I would become unfaithful to the greatest beauty of the century and to virtue itself for some little princess whose only merit was that she came from Paris. . . . Perhaps you believe that I love novelty, change, and people· from Paris as much as you do. You are sorely mistaken. I carry my chains with great pleasure and I would not exchange them for the kingdom of the Great Mogul.

. . . I cannot help telling you that I have spent the worst night in the world. . . . I saw you being unfaithful—that was the dream. It seemed to me that I had begged you not to see a certain tall man and that despite your promises you let him come to your room to say good-by. I was warned about it, and not being able to endure this infidelity, I pretended to have a letter from your mother to give you. I entered your bedroom abruptly and I saw the most awful sight in the world: This tall man was embracing you and what is worse you were alone in your room. You pretended to be a little angry with your Adonis, telling him that he was impertinent, and I wanted to leave, but you called me. I was delighted by that because it gave me the opportunity to whisper to you that you were the most ungrateful of women and that this would be the last time I would speak to you. And in fact I went to find Monsieur de Pude to ask him to send me to Hungary, which he did. I ask your pardon for this criminal dream. . . .

Königsmark was aware that he had lost favor with the Elector, but just as he feared the worst—that he would be given a leave that would send him away from Hanover— he was saved by an unexpected event: Denmark, allying herself with Sweden, prepared to invade the duchy of

Celle. The pretext was the fortifications raised by the Duke of Celle at a frontier town. The untimely zeal of a Danish general brought about the bombardment of the town and caused hostilities to break out. The Danes camped on the banks of the Elbe and Königsmark was named commander of the troops that were to prevent the enemy from crossing the river. He camped at Altenburg, from where his letters were dated until September 1693.

August 20, 1693

. . . My duty, my orders, and the small number of officers we have are the reasons why I haven't a moment's peace. I am writing you between ten and eleven at night. At midnight we return to guard duty, which will last until morning. From three to seven I sleep. At seven the Field Marshal comes to give me work for the rest of the day. You can see for yourself if I have the time to write you the long letters I want to write.

August 21, 1693

. . . Since midnight the night before last I have been constantly on horseback and I have ridden more than twelve leagues without setting foot on the ground. Nothing has happened yet. We talk to the Danes because there is only the river between us.

O tanto de la guerra,[7] let us talk of love. . . .

August 27, 1693

. . . When I am night and day on patrol I can think as much as I want. I see you always before me, and I

---

[7] Oh, enough about the war.

visualize you from head to toe and find it all perfect. If one can go on loving in the other world, I assure you that all the beauties there will not move me.

September 1, 1693

I must tell you that I wrote you two letters addressed to 131 [von Metsch], whom I thought was in Celle. I must know whether you have received them. Three letters were addressed to the postmaster at Celle. The one dated the 20th is the 9th letter, that dated the 26th is the 12th letter, and the one dated the 30th is the 14th letter. Look and see also whether you have the 13th letter. Please don't fail to reply about all this, you can attend to everything else later, for I am quite sure that I have been precise this time. It will surprise you to see me indulging in such thoughts considering the state I am in, but we have so much misfortune, my dear, that we must not create more ourselves. . . . Let us love one another eternally and let us once again swear, with a constancy that will never end, to live together.

. . . *The 3rd.* . . . I thought I would have an apoplectic fit when I opened your letter without seeing your handwriting. I had hoped to hear that you were better, but you say the contrary. . . . Do not believe that I am angry that you did not pen the letter, far from it, and I beg you to continue. . . . I am constantly on my knees praying that you recover completely, and I flatter myself that the Lord will finally have pity on me. My prayers are too pious not to be fulfilled. . . . I don't know when I will be able to do it, but my intention is to pretend that I am having a bout of fever. I will tell the Good Man that I would like to spend three days in 317 [Lüneburg] so that the fever does not take hold; and to take medicine.

Instead of staying at 317 I will take the mail coach and fly to Celle. I could spend two nights with you. What joy, what satisfaction. I could be at your feet bathing them with tears and you will see to what a pitiful state your illness has reduced me. . . . The sickness is increasing from day to day. My old lieutenant C. and two other lieutenants have fallen ill today. I don't know how I manage to escape it. It is a miracle.

At the Altenburg camp Königsmark wrote more and more desperate letters. He knew that the Electoral Prince was with his wife. If he gave her a child, Königsmark would have no alternative to drowning himself in the Elbe.

On May 19, 1693 he wrote:

It is now eight weeks since I left Hanover. I am fasting and live like a Capuchin monk. I don't miss a sermon and I no longer trim my beard. . . . Ah! If I could see those eyes happy to see me die before them. If I could kiss that little place which has given me so much pleasure. . . . At night, your portrait is before my eyes and on my lips and I am no longer a Capuchin.

. . . If I were quite sure that you wished to flee with me when the Danes cross the Elbe, I think I would let them cross . . . but, my angel, if it came to that point I think you would not be as prompt to accept it as you propose now, because one has got to earn a livelihood, that is the great obstacle.

Except for three insignificant fragments, the last letter, according to Schnath, was written in November 1693.

From that moment on, everything has disappeared.

Letters of Sophia Dorothea after the originals
belonging to the University of Lund (Sweden) and to
the Secret Archives of Berlin

From Einbeck Sophia Dorothea wrote:

March 1692

. . . If something can make me bear your absence without dying of grief it is the hope of showing you by my conduct that no one has ever loved as I love you and that nothing is the equal of my fidelity. It is proof against every test, and whatever may happen nothing in the world will be able to take me away from what I adore. Yes, my dear child, my passion can only end with my life.

I was so changed and depressed today that the Reformer [George Louis] took pity on me and said that he could well see that I was ill and that I ought to take care of myself. He is right, but my illness comes only from loving, and I never want to be cured. I have seen no one worth mentioning. I visited the Roman lady [Princess Sophia] for a while and I returned home as soon as I could to have the pleasure of talking about you. . . .

It is 8 o'clock and I must go pay my court. Good God, how silly I shall seem. I shall withdraw as soon as I have supped to have the pleasure of reading your letters. It is the only pleasure I shall have in your absence. Farewell, my adorable child, only death can take me from you because no human power will ever succeed in doing so. . . .

Sunday, June 12, 1692 from Hanover

. . . I deluded myself into thinking that I would see you

again after the review. I could have done so freely as the Reformer [George Louis] was absent. This fantasy made me spend two nights at the window, and I thought everyone who passed was you. The Governess [Mlle. de Knesebeck] kept telling me it was not so, but I did not wish to listen to reason. But I must tell you what I have done today: I retired right after dinner. In the evening there was music and the Awkward Heart [Sophia Dorothea] played with Colt [Sir William Colt, the British charge d'affaires]. . . . The Roman lady [Princess Sophia] talked a great deal about your handsomeness and the regularity of your features. I fear that others will find this only too true and that it will cost me many more tears.

I must end this. It is 3 o'clock and I am going to bed. Never doubt my fidelity; it is inviolable and I wish to live and die all yours.

Brockhausen, June 22

When I think that I will be four or five months without seeing you I fall into a melancholy that I cannot hide. A thousand sad thoughts overcome me, and I fear that we will be separated and that obstacles will be put in the way of my happiness. I see myself on the brink of a precipice. Indeed, if you knew the state I am in you would pity me. . . . scarcely was I dressed before I had to dine. Then I went to see the Pedagogue [the Duchess of Celle] for a while. . . . The Scold [the Duke of Celle] came to see me and showed me much kindness. I played with Chauvet and Madame de Beauregard. After supper I retired without having talked to anyone.

Good night. I am going to bed. How sad the nights are since your departure! I cannot think of the pleasures

I had with you and of my present state without mortal pain. Be constant, my dear child, all the happiness of my life hangs on it. For my part, I only want to live for you.

Sunday, June 10

. . . I have just received a letter from the Prince, who is allowing me to go to Brockhausen. He does not want me to stay there long because, he says, the Electress had given you a ribbon bow for your standard, and the ladies had done the same. Here are the very words of his reply: "You must really lack news to speak to me about the romantic life of my mother. I do not doubt that you have followed her example."

Brockhausen, Tuesday (June 13/23)

I arrived with the Electress from Brockhausen very late last night, and had the joy of finding your letter. I have reread it at least ten times and I would have answered it before going to bed if I could have. But before answering you I must tell you what happened at Brockhausen. We arrived there Sunday at 9 o'clock. First we had supper, and then everyone retired to his own room. I stayed with my mother and father until 2 [o'clock?]. They agreed fully with my grievances and are not at all pleased with the way I am being treated. My mother is exactly as I want her to be and if my father were too I would have nothing more to wish for.

The Prince has written a very civil letter to my father, leaving him absolutely free to keep me as long as he pleases. You know that he wrote me the contrary. I told my father so and he wants me to ask him how long I can stay. Let me know if you approve of this. I spent half of Monday alone in my bed and the other half with the Electress, my father, and my mother.

I would lose the faculty of speech without the Electress and Knesebeck, who are the only people with whom I have any conversation. We left at 7 and arrived at 11. I had supper in my room alone. I took a bath this morning to have a pretext for not going out. I have seen no one and I will not go out at all today. There is the precise account of everything I did yesterday and today.

Now I must answer your letter. I am sorry if my letter grieved you as much as you say it did, but I was so vexed with you that if I had wished to tell you all that my anger inspired me to say you would [not] have gotten off so lightly. I am satisfied with all your reasons and it is sufficient that you assure me that it is only a diplomatic move. Still, I would give my blood that you hadn't done it. Don't take offense, but how with your intelligence can you compare Monsieur Colt's ball, which I did not attend until two weeks after your departure and then only because the Elector and Electress were going, with the one in question which—that this makes me despair—took place only two hours after I left and after you had bid me such a tender farewell? The last thing I expected to learn was that you were at a party. But let us talk no more about it. I love you, and it is not even in my power to be angry for long. Before you wrote you were already pardoned.

Wednesday, June 14

The Electress talks about you every time I go for a walk with her, because as I have told you I am always alone with her. I don't know if she does it because of affection for you or to please me. In either case, she speaks of you a lot and I cannot even hear the sound of your name without a surge of emotion which I cannot control. She praises you so highly and with such pleasure that if she were younger I could not help being jealous, for really I think she is fond of you. She could not give me more evidence of it than she does. It even makes me uncomfortable.

Sophia Dorothea did not understand that the Electress's only object was to discover her daughter-in-law's secret.

Friday (June 16/26)

. . . I will begin with what is dearest to my heart, which is the desire to see you. I have already told you that it is quite easy as far as I am concerned, for Knesebeck lives in the small room near mine. You can come in by a rear door and you can stay for twenty-four hours if you wish without the least risk. As for me, every evening Knesebeck and I walk together under the trees near the house. We will wait for you from 10 o'clock to midnight. You know the usual signal. You must make yourself known by it. The gate in the fence is always open. Don't forget that you must give the signal and that I shall wait for you under the trees.

June 23

I am very worried because I still have received no letters from you. I am waiting for them impatiently, and I am dying to know how everything is going with you. I had a [letter] today from the Prince. It was an answer to what I wrote him from Lintzburg about the fact that they wanted to have Prince Max stay near me. I told him also that you were going to the Rhine. Here are his own words: "You have acted like a real Lucretia towards Prince Max, and I am beginning to see that honor is entirely safe in your hands. I astonished to learn that Königsmark is going to take part in the Rhine campaign. It will do him no good here since he has not yet paid his debts and from what people are saying he could get into trouble on that account."

I am very distressed about this and in addition to my sadness at not seeing you it is putting me in a very bad mood. Tell me what you want me to answer; I am convinced the Prince is taking a malicious delight in this because I know that he is full of envy and hatred for everyone who is charming and who has merit and distinction as you do.

I have been taken up only with my own plans. My mother is planning a deal which will be quite good if it succeeds.

She wants the Parliament of Celle to make me a present of 30,000 écus. She has spoken about it to Bernstorff, who has promised to spare no effort.

Bernstorff has shown me much friendship . . . and said that we need only call on him. He wants to come and see me, and I think you will be willing.

I am sure that if I could get Bernstorff on my side my father would do everything we wished. We must try in every way. The matter is too close to my heart to neglect it, for on it depends all the happiness of my life.

Wednesday, June 28

I am in despair that you are not as satisfied with me as you should be, because if I did not mention that I had spoken with Prince Max it was because I hadn't yet done so. I saw him only on the last day. You are wrong to believe that I had the least conversation with him. Here, word for word, is what I said: "Maxel, I thank you for the courtesy you showed me at Lintzburg."

He answered that it was only his duty and that he would always be glad to serve me in every way. I washed my mouth.

Bernstorff was there and my mother was on the other side, quite nearby. I can swear to you that he said nothing else and that the conversation ended there. The same evening he took leave of my father. My mother was holding my hand. She kissed him and wanted me to do the same. But I left her abruptly and went to the other side of the room. Then I asked Prince Max in a loud voice to convey my respects to the Electress. My mother begged my pardon for what she had done. I begged her never to do it again because it grieved me. She promised.

. . . Nothing is more innocent than my conduct, yet it seems to me you are not as convinced of my sincerity as you ought to be, and that you do not believe that I left my mother abruptly when she wanted me to kiss Prince Max. However, I assure you on pain of eternal damnation that that is what I did and that I moved several steps away. She asked my pardon later because she realized that she had hurt me. I am not at all surprised that you would not approve of this behavior; I find it as extraordinary as you do, but do not fear that she will ever be able to make me do anything which might displease you. I would a thousand times rather quarrel with her than fail the least little bit in what I owe you. Please be convinced of this, I beg you, and don't conjure up idle fancies over nothing.

My mother and my father are completely reconciled and are on better terms than ever. . . .

I do not despair of getting what I want, and I shall

never give up the game, for even if they refuse me I shall not be discouraged. But I find the circumstances most unfavorable to my plan: they talk of nothing but war and the difficulties we are in. It seems to me that we must wait for a more favorable moment.

My father is more affectionate to me than ever, and my mother overwhelms me with kindness.

Apart from the behavior that you do not like I am most content with her. Every day she gives me fresh assurances that everything she has is for me, and I am at rest on that score. Would to God that my father spoke in the same way. Today my father is terribly worried: The Danes are advancing and have everything they need to cross the Elbe. That will put more distance between us. Everything unites to make me despair. In the present state of affairs I do not dare press my father about what you know, for if things took a turn for the worse there would be nothing [left] for him. . . .

The lovers, who had up to now recognized the folly of fleeing, were so spurred by their passion and their suffering and their repeated separations (one of which lasted more than six months) that they lost all sense of reality and thought of nothing but extorting from the Duke of Celle the dowry which the Princess would need to live abroad with her "Chevalier."

Brockhausen, June 25-July 8, 1692

The Pedagogue and the Scold overwhelm me with kindness, which is most reassuring. They have not spoken to me about the Chevalier [Königsmark] since the day I arrived. I am surprised but I hope that they believe what I told them. I learned yesterday of the death of La Court's brother. It was a shock for I thought of the

Chevalier. He was healthy, he was young, and yet he is dead. You cannot imagine the sad reflections that causes me. I fear for you more than ever. If you truly love me, take care of yourself for my sake. What would become of me without you? . . . It is a fact that I have never loved you so tenderly and so perfectly. I am sensitive beyond imagining about everything that touches you.

I delight in talking to no one. The Scold and the Pedagogue feel obliged to me. They believe that it is to be with them that I flee everyone, and they do not know that it is to better show my passion and my attachment for you.

Brockhausen, July 7/17
. . . We are leaving tomorrow for Celle. I hope to find some letters from you there, and I am sorely in need of them to relieve me of my present anxiety. I haven't a moment of peace. I tremble lest I be betrayed, but what I fear most of all is your violent temper which never allows you time to reflect, and will lead you to abandon me without even finding out if I am guilty. My uncertainty is driving me to despair and I have never suffered so much. Tomorrow I shall know what to expect.

If I find nothing, I am lost. Farewell. Never has anyone loved more than I love you. My passion grows every day and I would die rather than lose you.

July 13/23
. . . I am glad my memory is better than yours, for if it should once fail me you are the man to pick a quarrel about nothing. . . .

... The coquetry you accuse me of is driving me to despair. I renounced that forever in giving myself to you. ...

... I had no doubt that I was betrayed and that Perspective [Countess Platen] had something to do with it. Yet even though I would have been lost forever if it had been true, I can swear to you that I never even thought about it, and that you alone were the cause of my worry. I feared losing you and I would rather have died. I trembled lest in your first rage you would enlist in the service of the Elector of Bavaria. And if you had done so I would have had to resolve never to see you again. Nothing equals the grief this thought caused me.

At C. [Celle] July 15/25

I do nothing but read your letter. Everything in it pleases me including your rage and your fantasies. But spare your beautiful hair, it is too nicely curled that you should do it any harm.

I have just had a terrible fright. The Pedagogue just came in although I left orders that I wished to sleep. The only thing I could do was turn my sheet of paper over. I was so scared that she might want to see what I was writing that I became pale and began to tremble. She asked me if I were ill and only stayed a moment. My heart is still racing and I have not recovered yet. ...

... I could not sleep all night. You occupied me more agreeably than sleep. ...

Never has a man been so truly and so tenderly loved as you.

... The Piedmontese Count whom you are so worried

about upsets me, and I cannot prevent myself from speaking to you about him again, although he is not worth the trouble. I swear to you again that I have not had the least conversation with him, nor even the least desire to speak to him. You should be ashamed to worry about people who are not worth looking at. You should know yourself better and you are so far superior to all other men that you should not fear any of them. . . .

Celle, July 16
. . . I got into bed after finishing my letter. I was reading all of yours and I thought myself safe because I had left word that I was asleep. The Pedagogue came to surprise me for the second time. All the Confidante could do was hide them under my blanket. I did not dare move for fear the paper would rustle. Finally the Pedagogue went away, to my great pleasure, for I was dying of fright. I hate all these surprises, but it is impossible to avoid them. . . .

Celle, July 18
. . . I am dying to see you with your beard, and I would give some of my blood to spend two hours with you. . . .

At Celle, July 20/30
. . . I do not know what conclusion I must draw from your silence. I am surprised by it and cannot imagine the reason for it. Today I received a letter from the Reformer [George Louis], and I am in despair that he should write more regularly than you. What has become of your eagerness? Does the Brussels air inspire this

coldness in you or has a new passion already entirely erased me from your memory? Whatever I do to reassure myself on this point I cannot control myself and I am terribly afraid I have guessed correctly. I beseech you, do not force yourself to write me any more if you cannot do it willingly. Doubtless you have more agreeable occupations and it would be unkind to deprive you of them. I want your inclinations to rule all your actions with regard to me. I cannot reconcile myself at all to everything you do just for the sake of decorum. I confess I am most piqued by your indifference: I do everything I can to excuse you, but I cannot succeed, and I have never been so deeply affected. . . .

. . . I find a passage in your letter which does not please me at all. Here are your own words: "Only the danger to which I see you exposed could make me dream of leaving you, because since there is no hope that we may ever live together, why should we risk ourselves for so little, that is to say for seeing each other twenty times a year?"

What a fine reason for abandoning me! Is that love? Do you still love me or are you looking for a pretext for leaving me? I tremble for it because you cannot believe that I could change. You know yourself. You are the most lovable of all men and it is impossible that I could dream of anything after you.

The letters arrived almost daily. When they were late, Mlle. de Knesebeck interfered and wrote to Königsmark. Here is an example:

Try to reassure the Princess I beg of you. She is extremely worried about your faithfulness and she is fearful of losing you by an inconstancy. All day she does nothing else but sometimes weep, sometimes complain, and then sigh. Do not think that I am against you, but I admit that she affects me deeply. Farewell, my dear. You are much in the wrong not to have written. What do you want us to conclude from that?

Still, Mlle. de Knesebeck appears to have had flashes of farsightedness, for she warned the Princess of the danger of these letters. The Prudent Governess advised against writing too precise accounts of the Princess's comings and goings because the details would betray her. One letter disappeared and none of the three knew what happened to it.
One night Sophia Dorothea wrote to her lover:

I was interrupted at this point in the most terrible way in the world. I thought I was perfectly safe because I had left word that I was sleeping. I had your portrait right near me attached to a screen and . . .

[*the end of the letter has disappeared*].

. . . I don't think that I can make [Prince Max, Sophia Dorothea's young brother-in-law] move out. I have no excuse for it, because our apartments are quite separate and communicate only by a door which I need only keep closed. Moreover, all my women are around me so that I fear I shall not succeed.

. . . Since the counts have gone you no longer have a pretext for coming openly, and I cannot see how the thing is possible otherwise. I am opposed to your coming in disguise. It seems to me too dangerous and as you say it might ruin our affair forever. . . . I would be most unfair to oppose your trip to Holl [Holland], yet I do not believe you will have the time for it because the Danes are still advancing and have everything they need to maintain a siege, so we are all very worried.

At C. [Celle] July 28, August 7
. . . It was most obliging of you not to go to Brussels, yet do not restrain yourself. I don't wish to be an inconvenience, and as long as you keep your heart for me I shall be too happy and pleased. But keep it for me entirely and do not allow anyone in the world to contest it, because surely I would die of that.

July 29/August 8
When I woke up I heard that a terrible battle was being fought and that you were part of it, so you can imagine my anguish. I am terribly worried and agitated and I will not rest until I know that you are out of all danger. My state is worthy of pity. I imagine that every shot is aimed at you and that you alone must endure all the dangers of this affair. Good God, what would become of me if anything happened to you? I would not be able to control myself and I would leave here to come and give you all the care necessary and never leave you again.

As a true woman in love, Sophia Dorothea did not realize that she was asking a professional soldier to dishonor himself by not going to war:

. . . I beseech you not to expose me in the future to worries like this. Never leave me again, I beg of you, and if it is true that you love me, do yourself a favor and spend the rest of your life with me.

How I hate King William, who is the cause of all this. He gives me mortal pain by endangering all that I adore.

August 1/11

I want to scold you for having exposed yourself unreasonably and unnecessarily. You want to make me despair with your nonchalance. Ought you not to keep yourself safe for me?

I would be in despair should you do anything to dishonor yourself, but I cannot pardon you for acting like a foolish young man as you did.

I do not know what is wrong with the Elector's eyes to have found you ugly. If he had seen you with my eyes he would have found you charming, the most agreeable of men. I don't think anyone can dispute that, and whatever wonderful things you may tell me about the Duke of Richmond, I am convinced he would only pale in comparison to you.

. . . I have just been interrupted by the Scold and the Peda [gogue]. All I could do was hide what I was writing. What a treat they would have had if they had seen it. They are very kind, but they are always preaching me to live on good terms with the Reformer. The Scold will not hear jokes on this subject, which means that I don't dare speak to him about it as often as I would like. If you know how tired I am of not seeing you, you would never be so cruel as to leave me a second time.

I was born to love you and to be eternally yours. Good

night. I would give half my blood to hold you in my arms.

Friday 4

I spent the whole day in bed and went for a walk in the evening. .... I retired immediately after supper to have the pleasure of reading your letter. I spent two hours over it, and it has so woken me up that I don't think I shall be able to sleep.

Einbeck, August 12

Nothing worth mentioning has taken place and I have done nothing but drink, eat, and sleep since the trip. I think of you from morning till night. It is my sole occupation and the only one that pleases me.

I am told that you are losing your money. I am annoyed by it, but one can't be equally happy in everything and love must console you for gambling.

If you had arranged a special place for me to hide it would not be better than this one. It is away from all society and offers devastating solitude. At another time I would have been terribly bored here, because there is no one and the people with us are not at all amusing. However, because I know you it is a real pleasure to be cloistered like this and I would have despaired had there been people here, because you would not have failed to believe that I had come to seek them. It is certain that I know myself no longer and I don't understand how a person can have changed to the point I have. I dread society now as much as I liked it before, and all this to please you. But I have said to you a thousand times that I think only of you and count everything else as nothing.

. . . In everything you tell me there appears a coldness which chills me. I have been so concerned with justifying myself with regard to your unjust suspicions that I have not told you of the sadness that your cold behavior has caused me.

I am going to bed. Good night. You are the most charming of men, but you are never content.

. . . The mail arrived this morning; it is four o'clock and I have received nothing. I no longer dare expect anything today and I am ill at ease about it. I have not slept for the last several nights. You are too much in my mind and as soon as I want to go to sleep you appear to me with your charms and you wake me so completely that I can no longer think of sleep. You will find me thinner and not seeing you and not having any letters from you is no way to recover my *embonpoint.*

Luisburg, Thursday June 8, 93
I arrived in the saddest state in the world and all the torments you can imagine are nothing compared to what I suffered after having left you. I shall see you no more then and for three months I will be deprived of everything that makes the pleasure and charm of my life.

To crown my misery they wanted to put Prince Max next to me in the Reformer's bedroom. I hoped to go to bed when I arrived. I was so overcome with grief and had such a headache that I could not stand up. Imagine my astonishment to find everything in disorder because my servants had taken it upon themselves to prepare nothing before they knew my wishes. As I know your wishes and because the thing is impertinent in itself, I don't remember ever having been so angry. Everyone was at supper when I arrived. I sent word to the major-domo to change this fine arrangement because I absolutely refused to have it this way. He raised the most absurd objections and excused himself by saying it was ordered by Don Diego [the Elector]. Finally I got Nopstein up from the table to come to me. You would have been most satisfied with me because I spoke in a very loud voice. He spoke to Don Diego and returned to say that if the apartment were three times as large it would be for me alone. At the same time he gave orders that Colin [Prince Max] should stay in the other house. Colin was most polite, from what I heard.

October 10
Yet I have never deserved your affection more than I do now. Whatever sermon I must endure and whatever fear they may try to inspire in me, nothing shakes the resolution I have made to love you eternally and to prove it to you as much as I can. They can stop me from seeing you but they will never stop me from being yours all my life. You can be sure of it: You take the place of everything. Some one told D. Diego that the Chevalier had only changed houses in order to put up the adventuress [Aurora von Königsmark] and by this means attract the Awkward Heart [Sophia Dorothea].

I avoid everyone. I speak to no one. I worry about the merest trifles, and hardly have I left than you forget everything you promised me and console yourself with women who hate me to the death. No, nothing can excuse you and nothing in the world can be so unkind. Good God, what will it be like in a few months, since you are so easily comforted on the very day I leave? I cannot say more, for my tears prevent me.

The Princess had found out that on the day of her departure Königsmark had gone to a reception at the Countess Platen's.
She made him a classic scene of jealousy.

Saturday
I have not slept at all and my eyes are as big as fists. I don't dare show myself. Poor Knesebeck is pale because I fret so. She sleeps in the small room next to mine and I woke her at 5 in the morning. I am still in bed, in despair at what you have done to me. It shows so little tenderness that I cannot be comforted. I expected nothing of the kind. A thunderbolt would have surprised me less. I don't dare tell you all I think of you.

Farewell, Monsieur, I wish you all the pleasures in the world and I do not doubt that you will find new ones every day.

. . . Therefore do not restrain yourself, I entreat you. Think only of your pleasures and count me as nothing. I do not doubt that all these parties will end with a complete reconciliation between you and the Platen woman, or some new love. Lacking that, happiness, the spice of all pleasures, cannot be perfect. If you only need my good wishes to contribute to your happiness, you have them entirely that there is no joy that I do not wish you. It so happens that fortune, to give me a chance at revenge, has sent here today a young Baron from Mayence who

134

is very handsome and quite magnificent. You will no doubt willingly let me look after him so that I don't die of boredom. I believe you are still too much a friend to refuse me this little *consolation*. You can see that I am more sincere than you because although you sent me a word about your party you tell me nothing about the ladies, nor that the Platen woman was to have been there. And yet the whole thing was given for her. I am well repaid for living like a hermit and avoiding everyone, including people of sixty. But that's enough, and I will say no more. If you thought a little about my behavior and about yours toward me you ought to be ashamed of acting as you do.

I will not reproach you; you ought to reproach yourself, but it makes me realize that there is very little love that is proof against absence. Unfortunately for me my love does not diminish and I feel if anything too much tenderness and sensibility. Teach me how to become indifferent like you.

Wednesday (July 19/29)

. . . You seem very phlegmatic about what I do, and I assure you that I am not less so about everything concerning you. I am most happy to be in this mood because otherwise I would have been very hurt by the party you gave last night for the Platen woman and the other ladies. Stubenfol gave an account of it at table which charmed everyone. It was felt that nothing could have been better arranged and that everything showed civility and gallantry. I am not at all surprised that you surpassed yourself, the objects of your attention were well worth the trouble, and when one is inspired by so much charm, one always succeeds perfectly. I must say that I

have no trouble following your advice and that I am
quite content to stay here as long as it pleases you. Many
thanks for all the news you give me. . . . I also send a
thousand good wishes for the continuation of your
pleasures and I assure you that I would be most distressed to interrupt them by my presence. I do not know
how you wish me to reconcile the eagerness you have to
know what I am doing with the indifference you display
in your conduct, because if you had the least affection and
consideration for me you would not behave toward me as
you do. You are at a continual round of parties . . . and
all of these are surrounded by such displeasing circumstances that it is hard to imagine anything worse. But
it would be wrong of me to complain and find fault
with your conduct: It is charming toward me and denotes
a surprising tenderness and fidelity. It is my own
conduct that you could rightly criticize: Every day, you
tell me, I go to the theater where people whisper in my
ear and coax me until the lights go up. You make up
these stories to fill your paper, because there is not a
word of truth in them. There have been only two performances in the theater since I have been here and each
time I was in my father's box alone with him, only
opening my mouth to answer him.

. . . I trust Bernstorff only as much as I should. My
mother presses him every day so that Parliament hasten
to give me 30,000 écus, but I believe that this wretched
war will delay the matter.

*Prince Max was a continuous leitmotif. He figured in
more than twenty letters. Königsmark's jealousy was so
idiotic that he himself was amazed at it and asked himself how he could be jealous "of this ape." These two*

lovers who were dying for each other and had fewer and fewer opportunities to see each other, sacrificed the opportunities they did have, for behind the door that separated Prince Max's apartment from the Princess's, the Prince (who would never have dreamt of it) might make "little holes" and watch her change her clothes and show herself "stark naked"! And Sophia Dorothea even took the lead in this race to absurdities. She so feared the reproaches of Philipp Christoph that she made scenes of alarmed modesty which evoked an ironic response from the whole ducal family, beginning with her husband, who sarcastically congratulated this new Lucretia.

Friday (June 30)

. . . Yesterday I witnessed a conversation between my father and my mother which gave me much food for thought. You could not imagine anything more unkind nor more bitter than what they said to each other. . . . I trembled to see people whom love alone united become so exasperated over so little, to the point that they threatened to leave each other. They finally made it up after two hours, but my mother is stung to the quick by my father and she is right. You may imagine how little power she has since she cannot succeed in an affair that she has so much to heart. This does not give me much hope for my own affairs, for all my hopes were pinned on my mother and I see that she only needs to wish for a thing for it not to be done. My father is incredibly hard. I am not at all impressed by him because I have learned from his behavior toward my mother that one should not count on his kindness. So I am in a very bad mood today. . . .

July 1
If I had not received a letter from 205 [Madame de Harli] before receiving yours I believe yours would have given me a féver by speaking of your pleasures and that of the ladies with whom you played. But thanks to her I am free of anxiety. Here is what she wrote: "Yesterday all the ladies were there, but they must have been very dull because I saw our courtiers languishing and not at all busy. One must be really tired of pleasures to be reduced to playing with children, as Königsmark did all evening. He spent his time making houses of cards for the little princess and the little chevalier. I was grateful to him, but besides that he seemed anxious not to give his mistress cause for jealousy, if he has a mistress. Handsome and well built as he is, it seems more likely than not that he does have one."

August 5
What misfortune, good God, and what shame to love you without being loved! Yet that is my fate: I was born to love you and I shall continue to love you as long as I live. If it is true that you have changed toward me, as I have a thousand reasons to fear, I want no other punishment for you than that you never find, wherever you are, passion and fidelity equal to mine. Despite the pleasures you will find in making fresh conquests, I wish that you may never be able to help regretting the feelings and affection I have for you. You will never find them anywhere in the world to be so tender and so sincere.

I love you more than anyone has ever loved and with an unequaled sensitivity. But I tell you the same things too often and you must be heartily sick of them. Don't take it badly, I implore you, and do not begrudge me the only consolation I have, which is to complain to you of your own hardness. I am so hurt by it that nothing else moves me. Yet I should be very anxious that despite everything we have done to discover the whereabouts of the letter you wrote to me at Zell [Celle], we have not received a word in reply. Everything seems to conspire to overwhelm me: You perhaps no longer love me and I see myself on the eve of being absolutely lost. It is too much grief all at once, and I will break down under it. I must end. . . . Farewell, I forgive you everything that you make me suffer.

My God, if you abandon me I no longer wish to live. What would I do in the world if you no longer loved me? I am only here for you. I owe you many thanks for your charming behavior toward me, but I fear that if you irritate the Platen woman too much she will revenge herself. Humor her a little, but not too much. I am in despair at my excessive delicacy and I know perfectly well that it will work against me, but I love you so passionately that I can't be reasonable.

With the illogic of women in love, the Princess urged her lover to humor the all-powerful Countess Platen and go to see her, and then reproached him for having gone:

I am sorry that you no longer go to the Countess Platen's. It it is quite important. The other shrew worries me less.

Don't be silly enough to stop going to Platen's. You absolutely must humor her and I beseech you with all my love to go there as before.

Monday (July 17/27)

I pity you with all my heart for being as you are. If I knew a medicine that would cure you I would dispense it with true joy even if it were to cost me all my blood. But tell me yourself what I must do to reassure you about all your fantasies. I don't think I have forgotten anything in this regard. If I could reproach myself with having neglected the least thing I would not forgive myself, but it seems to me that no one could do more than I have done. I hardly dare tell you that I have spent the entire night without sleeping for fear that you will not believe it and that you will ridicule me again. Nonetheless, nothing in the world is more true.

I am wounded to the bottom of my heart by your continual suspicions. You want me to pity you and I am a thousand times more to be pitied than you. If you knew how awful it is to be suspected when one is innocent you would see that there are no more terrible tortures than those you make me suffer. If I saw an end to these suspicions and this lack of trust, and if I could imagine a way of curing you of them, my life would seem of little account.

I cannot imagine that you could do away with them. You are not the master of them, and the least thing that has any connection with your fantasies revives your jealousy, your suspicions, and your distrust more than ever. I am not angry with you; I pity you, because I see that you cannot master yourself. But I find that nothing in the world is more miserable than I. You cannot possibly love me as I so wish you would as long as you remain in the state of uncertainty in which you appear to be.

I cannot live this way, always suspected, always

accused of lacking sincerity and of subterfuge—and this
by the person who is most dear to me and who ought to
do me more justice.

I tremble that all these beautiful fantasies will finally
destroy your affection. It is impossible that it should
persist with the feelings I see you prey to.

Yesterday I read my marriage contract, which could
not be more disadvantageous to me than it is.

The Prince is the absolute master of everything and
nothing belongs to me. Even the allowance he ought to
give me is so badly explained that they can easily quibble
over it. I was very much surprised by all this because
I did not expect it at all. It hurt me so much that I had
tears in my eyes.

. . . My mother behaves in the most honorable way in
the world to me and I am angry that you should call her
a madwoman, for I have never loved her as much as
yesterday and today. Perhaps all this will be a matter
of complete indifference to you because I do not know
whether I can hope that a little affection remains.
From the way in which your letter is phrased, I have
considerable cause to doubt it.

At 1 o'clock after midnight
A moment after I was dressed my mother came to see me
to suggest a carriage ride. She called Stubenfol, who was
in the antechamber, to show him how I am lodged. I
assure you I would have given a great deal if he had been
transformed into a handsome and well-built Marquis.
The resentment I feel made me regret that he was only a
stupid creature because this can give you no worry, and
I am so peeved that I would be delighted to make you
worry. . . .

Saturday (July 22/August 1)
I expected you to appease me with an infinity of excuses and the most beautiful things in the world. I was much deceived to find that on the contrary you are acting the proud one instead of asking my pardon. I could not help laughing to see that you fell into my trap and that my Baron sticks in your throat. Your anger makes me so happy that I have forgotten how angry I should be at you. I am charmed to have revenged myself all on my own and I like myself a thousand times better for it. I hope you will be free of anxiety before receiving this, for I have drawn you a portrait of the person concerned, and that is enough.

Monday July 30
My mother has replied to me about Max. Here are her own words: "I advise you not to be embarrassed that he is so close. If the neighbor makes too much noise you have only to move your bed into the antechamber. In that way you will avoid the noise and remove yourself from the suitor." Tonight I shall know what to do. My mother also tells me that the Electress has thanked her for allowing me to return, and that she was charmed to see me. My mother replied on that point what she told me, which is that considering all the kindness the Electress shows me, it is right and proper for me to leave my father and her to pay my court to her. . . .

At 11 o'clock
I have seen the Platen woman and we had a three-hour tête-a-tête. The most important part of the conversation was that she knows the Electress lectured me about you

more than a year ago and that far from the Elector having
spoken to the Electress, as the Electress would have had
me believe, it was the Electress who had driven him
crazy about it. She said that the Elector had never talked
to the Electress about it, and that afterwards the Electress
told a number of people how she had warned me to
change my conduct toward you because it was doing me
harm. Platen then urged me to change my ways; that the
life I lead is so retiring that everyone wonders at it; that
people complain that I neither look at nor speak to anyone; that I cannot imagine all they were saying, because
they do not think it natural for a woman of my age to
renounce everything so completely, and they are seeking
the reason for it. I replied that if I had singled out
someone and had not treated everyone the same way,
people would have a right to complain, but that as I talk
to no one everyone should be satisfied and that they were
wrong to complain since I treated everyone alike. She
spoke several times about you; she is only too pleased to
do so. At the end we parted as close friends and never
was friendship confirmed by as many pledges as she
made. I have not left my bedroom today and my diary
will soon be brought up to date. I am going to bed, for
I need it. I do not sleep and I am worn out. But how
can I sleep when I have a big boy like you in my head?

Friday

Since you want me to believe that your party was a
serious affair and that everyone went home very early,
I have to believe you, although Stubenfol said that
people had never been so merry and that the party did
not wind up until after midnight.

I don't want to think about it any more. . . . I want only to busy myself with all that you have told me of your affection. It tickles me, it delights me, it provides me with a pleasure I cannot really express. Continue having these charming feelings, they constitute all the happiness of my life. How I love you to be as amorous as you say you are: At the very thought that I could change your blood races and you are so agitated that you cannot continue! This passage charms me. It seems to me so tender and so natural that my passion redoubles. I have reread it twenty times and I cannot tire of it.

Brockhausen, July 3/13

. . . I am annoyed that you are displeased because I went to the Colt ball, but I could not avoid going, for he pressed me so insistently to come. The foreigners did not keep me in Hanover. They had left a few days before. I have already told you that I hardly talked to them at all and I have informed you exactly about everything I did. If you don't believe me, I am ready to swear it on the most terrible oath. I am incapable of deceiving you. I love you passionately and all the misfortunes in the world will never tear me from you. And yet you think that I am betraying you and you do not want to write any more. You reduce me to despair.

. . . I have received a note from the Electress on the subject you know about. Here is what she writes: "The Elector told me again the same things I told you yesterday: That it would be ridiculous not to come to Herrenhausen because of such unfounded scruples, and that he would answer for any slanders people might spread. He said that Max will not rape you, that you have only to close the door. Thus it rests with you to come when it pleases you. . . ." She adds to that much love. . . ·

September 2/12 1692

. . . This second of September it was so late when I wrote that I could not reply to everything you told me. I have reread your letter several times. It is a mixture of affection and gentle mockery which I find very pretty and it seems to me that whatever appearance you put on it, my trip does not please you. . . . I don't think I will go to the Frankfurt Fair, and I will not say a word to bring it about. It seems to me that this ought to persuade you that I am not seeking people out. . . . I hope to leave here in two weeks. The Pedagogue decided this today. I shall return with her to the Scold. . . . I still can tell you nothing positive concerning Gör, but I do not think I will go because the season is too advanced for the Reformer to be there. . . . I will be able to see you soon. I will judge your affection by your ardor, but I beg you to arrange matters so that I see you alone the first time. I could not endure seeing you in public, and my emotion would betray me. They say that the French could take us easily, which makes me want to leave very much, because I would not at all like to be captured. I want to keep your conquest for you.

September 13/23 1692, Wiesbaden

Instead of the extreme pleasure which all your letters give me, the one I received this evening cut me to the quick. I cannot imagine anything more offensive than what you write. . . . What moment of my life could have

earned me the opinion that you have of me? . . . Thank
God I feel that my heart is as noble as it ought to be.
I don't want to say anything more on this subject. I
might get angry and I really hate bitterness. But to
answer the four points you feel so strongly about, I was
completely mistaken if I wrote that Sparr has been at L.
and if I did not do so it is surely an oversight and because
I did not find that he was worth the trouble remember-
ing. . . . So far as the Fair is concerned, I assure you
that I did not say a word in order to go there, but as I am
honest I am willing to admit that I am not angry about it.
And as for my new lover [the Landgrave of Hesse], you
are mad to get upset about him because he is far away
and in all probability I shall not see him at all. . . . I am
convinced that he will not come to Hanover, but if he
should come I will be rude to him rather than endure
his visits—provided that I am more satisfied with you
than I am this evening. I am very silly to give you
answers about all your fantasies, you who are so little
concerned about me. . . . It is true that you later want
to make amends for your faults, but that is not enough,
and I am not content because I want your esteem and you
do not show any for me.

Frankfurt, September 14
I have been here for two hours. The Pedagogue went
to the Princess of Tarente's house where I saw only silly
people. From there we went to the Fair where I saw not
one person of quality. The Marionette [Duchess of
Saxony-Eisenach] and her sister-in-law are here. I
won't see them until tomorrow, which is nice because I
can get some rest, which I need because I didn't sleep
a wink last night. I spent half of it writing you and the

other half grieving about that fine passage in your letter. . . . I hope I will not see the Landgrave or anyone; I hope so with all my heart. . . . All the charms of your letter have not been able to make me forgive the offensive part. Don't worry about my conduct, which will be divine, I assure you.

6 / The Rosenkavalier Left No Traces

Sophia Dorothea and Philipp Christoph, or the Hunted Lovers. Why the hue and cry? Why was their adultery not the classic liaison accepted at courts and made honorable by the passage of time? The sort of situation in which the mother-in-law draws in her claws, the mother is complacent, the father-in-law quite content to see his son cuckolded, and the son himself, a little embarrassed by the quasi-marital life he leads with his mistress, buying peace with silence. These little German courts took as their model Versailles, which was crawling with mistresses and bastards. Why did not Hanover copy the Sun King in this? Why should this primitive drama have taken place among civilized people at the dawn of the most civilized of centuries?

It took place because a hateful, coldly perfidious monster, the Countess Platen, spied, eavesdropped, intercepted letters, and extended her web. She was the acknowledged mistress and uncontested beauty of the Hanoverian court, all-powerful with the Duke, accepted and even graciously treated by the Duchess (that superior woman was above such trifles). Yet the Countess lived without pleasure alongside the ravishing young Princess, whose rank and beauty eclipsed her. Madame Platen was the acknowledged mistress, certainly, but one must remember how frought such a situation would be with hidden mortifications, secret humiliations, veiled maneuvers, criminal desires. Outshone yet triumphant because she enjoyed the Elector's favor, Madame Platen might have ultimately accepted Sophia Dorothea. But then Königsmark came on the scene.

It is certain that Countess Platen loved him; that she tried to take him away from the Princess; that she passionately desired him as her lover, her son-in-law, her friend, or whatever he wished to be as long as he remained by her in her little court at Monplaisir. He took her, then rejected her, and finally humiliated her. She had her revenge.

In the heat of their passion, Sophia Dorothea and Königsmark clearly compromised themselves more and more, and revealing incidents came to light. The Platen woman used them for her own ends to put pressure on the Elector. She must have managed at times to hide her hatred because Palmblad quotes two most curious letters in which Sophia Dorothea speaks of the help Countess Platen gave her.

However that may be, the Elector summoned Königsmark and told him with much politeness and tact that his presence in Hanover was no longer so fervently desired as it once had been. Königsmark understood and, taking advantage of the fact that his friend August had just ascended the throne of Saxony, he asked for a leave of absence and went to Dresden to congratulate him.

The court of Saxony was emerging from a dreadful tragedy. The previous Elector, George IV, the elder brother of Ernst August, had begun to reign when he was twenty-five. He soon fell madly in love with a very beautiful Viennese, Mlle. Sybille von Niedschütz, whom he brought to Dresden along with her mother, the wife of General Niedschütz. These ladies immediately set about looting Saxony—its estates, its castles, its thalers. To put a stop to the scandal the Elector's mother, a daughter of the King of Denmark, decided to marry her son off. George consented, but installed his mistress next to him in the coach that took him to the frontier to meet his fiancée. Things came to such a pass that August in his turn reprimanded his elder brother the Elector George. The latter drew his sword in a fury, but he did not set upon his brother, whose strength he knew, but stabbed August's wife. August had no difficulty in overcoming George, carrying him off in his arms, and throwing him brutally onto his bed.

Rather ashamed and repentant, George IV yielded to his brother's wish to make a tour of Europe, and even fitted him out magnificently for it. This is how Ernst August, having met and made friends with Königsmark, took him to Venice, then to the Iberian peninsula and to France.

Meanwhile, Mlle. von Niedschütz, who had become Countess of the Empire von Röchlitz, consolidated her hold over the Elector. She even sought to become his second wife. George IV had agreed and had tried to overcome the resistance of his ministers on the grounds that nothing in the Old Testament forbade having two wives, quite the contrary. Happily, smallpox rid Saxony of this beautiful scourge in 1694. The Elector, mad with despair, clutched the corpse of his beloved in his arms and angrily refused to be separated from her. The people, believing their sovereign the victim of an evil spell, rioted and besieged the palace. Only then was the favorite given an almost royal funeral and buried behind the high altar of the Church of Saint Sophia.

After this final sacrilegious comedy, the Elector died in his turn, of smallpox, of course, leaving his people convinced that the sorceress had taken him with her.

Thus Ernst August became Elector of Saxony, to the great joy of his subjects. He had everything to please the crowd—very dark hair, very handsome, flashing eyes, and a strength that earned him the nickname of August the Strong, or the Hercules of the North. He was intelligent, goodhearted, and full of good intentions. Unfortunately he had in abundance those faults that make a monarch popular but which lead to his ruin: he was generous, lavish, a bon vivant, and loved women to excess.

He received his friend Königsmark with great joy, did not repay him the 30,000 thalers he owed him, but named him a general and gave him a command in his army.

Königsmark took part in all the coronation celebrations—the masquerades, the balls, the bear and wolf hunts, the regattas crewed by sailors in yellow satin, and the tournaments of men in medieval armor.

Königsmark had left during the first days of April 1694, and spent two months in Saxony. There are no letters dating from this period. Perhaps the lovers, appeased by the distance and calm after the storm, did not write. These two months in Dresden were a respite for Philipp Christoph, for he was much feted. At an officers' mess party in his honor Königsmark, who had drunk too much, was provoked by his friends who teased him about his good fortune. Thereupon he drew a caricature of the ladies at the court of Hanover, and in particular of the Platen woman. He would have done better to remember that the lady had her spies every-where, including Dresden, where she had placed a former chambermaid of Sophia Dorothea's, who had been ex-pelled from Hanover for misconduct. As he got drunker and drunker, Königsmark apparently alluded to his coming flight with the Electoral Princess. . . . If that is true, he had signed his death warrant. But one can exonerate him from this indiscretion. Such a statement would not have failed to figure in the reports of Stephney, the British envoy to the court of Dresden. But there is not a trace of it, and at that time the diplomat was not even aware of Königsmark's liaison with Sophia Dorothea.

Unfortunately, at this ill-fated banquet Königsmark did not limit himself to lampooning the faded charms of the Countess Platen, the devices she used to try to make herself look younger—her make-up, her milk baths. He also spoke about other women and in particu-larly offensive terms about Mélusine von Schulenburg.

The story got back to Hanover. The pacific Mélusine, for once most irritated, complained to George, who burst into his wife's room and reproached her for her conduct toward Königsmark. The Princess replied that by flaunt-ing Schulenburg he was himself the laughingstock of Europe. On this occasion the word divorce was used for the first time, and by Sophia Dorothea. The ordinarily phlegmatic George Louis became enraged, threw himself on his wife, and began tearing her hair.

Immediately after this quarrel Sophia Dorothea de-cided to return to her parents without asking her father-in-law's permission to leave Hanover. The Duke of Celle was most embarrassed to see his daughter and did not dare take her side, because he was hoping for Hanover's military support against the Danes. Sophia Dorothea fell ill and spent an entire month at Celle, looked after by her mother. Then she accompanied her parents to Brockhausen. Judging that she had been away long enough, her parents then forced her to return to Hanover. Father and daughter had some heated discussions which finally turned the Duke against the Princess. The Elector and Electress of Hanover, seeing that their son was gravely in the wrong, let it be known at Brockhausen that they would be happy to have their daughter-in-law return and that they would wait for her at Herrenhausen. To offer these honorable amends must certainly have been hard for the proud Electress. Herrenhausen was on the way to Hanover and for Sophia Dorothea not to stop there, under the circumstances, was worse than insolence; it was a challenge and a sort of public breach.

At Herrenhausen, they heard her coach approaching. . . . It did not stop. As her dumfounded parents-in-law watched, Sophia Dorothea continued coldly on her way.

Why did the lovers not burn their letters? Why did they move up the fatal day by writing too much? Their letters are still being read by inquisitive historians as they were by contemporaries with evil intentions.

While they were separated during the first months of 1694, did Sophia Dorothea and Königsmark write to each other? Were their letters more and more compromising? The fact that they returned to Hanover within two days of each other proves that they were communicating.

As bold as he was garrulous, Königsmark returned from Dresden at the end of June 1694. Hanover was forbidden to him, but with his habitual imprudence, he disregarded this. He was more or less a deserter, having without authorization acquired high ranks in two armies that were not allies, if not quite enemies. He threw caution to the wind, and was ruled only by his love. Thus he insisted that they both flee immediately to France. But everything thwarted his plans. On close inspection the problems seemed insurmountable. The principal one was the lack of money. Königsmark, the famous prodigal, was completely ruined, and Sophia Dorothea had been able to get nothing from her father. What would they live on in France? She would cease to be an influential German princess favorable to the French cause, and would become a Huguenot refugee as her mother once had been. Louis XIV no longer had anything to gain by treating her tactfully, and as Wilkins correctly noted, the Princess Palatine was the sworn enemy of her mother and would probably have had her barred from Versailles. Wolfenbüttel was a safer refuge: there were common memories, identical interests and discontents, and on the soil of an ally of Sweden, Königsmark would have made up with his king.

The subsequent course of this tragedy proves that Madame Platen knew everything. Even while closeted with each other in their apartments, the two lovers were surrounded by spies. The inquisitive Platen anticipated whatever they wanted to do. She was the first to throw herself into the great adventure, and her hatred inspired her to hatch a hateful scheme. On July 1, 1694, Königsmark received a penciled note from Sophia Dorothea asking him to come that very evening to her apartment in the palace between 11 o'clock and midnight. The door would be opened to him when he whistled their signal, the "Spanish Follies" set to music by Corelli. Later Sophia Dorothea asserted that this letter was a forgery.

When questioned, the faithful Knesebeck said it was genuine. The note was certainly authentic, but the Platen woman had known about it.

In borrowed clothes, Königsmark left his house without informing his servants and slipped through the gardens, certain that no one had seen him. He stood at the entrance of the castle. . . . (There is almost nothing left of Leinenschloss today, for half the city of Hanover was destroyed in World War II.) Philipp whistled the signal tune and saw Mlle. de Knesebeck appear at the back gate. She took him by the hand, led him upstairs and through a dark corridor to the Princess. The corridor was accessible at both ends, at one end by the little door that Königsmark used, while at the other end it gave access to the entrance of a huge formal salon, the Hall of the Knights.

Thus he came into Sophia Dorothea's room, whose windows looked over the river Leine. It was a very hot night and the stars were blurred by the mist.

Madame Platen was informed as soon as the lovers were together. She ran to the Elector, told him what was happening, roused him, and with great difficulty got him to order Königsmark's arrest. Wilkins says that at this point the Elector was resolved to go himself to the apartment of his daughter-in-law, but that Platen dissuaded him. Perhaps she mistrusted the instinctive kindness and indecisiveness of this feeble old man. The anonymous author of the *Histoire secrette* is of another opinion. He relates that the Elector did go in person and took an active part in the tragedy. The most common version is that the Elector allowed his mistress to wring an arrest warrant from him and put three (or four) halberdiers at the disposal of this fury.

Having given the assassins something to drink, and

sworn them to secrecy under pain of death by hanging, Platen concealed them under the huge mantelpiece in the great hall, ordering them to wait in its shadow and pounce on anyone she pointed out to them. In the silence of the night, the soldiers dozed off. A ray of light shone from under the door leading into the Princess's apartment. . . . Knesebeck kept watch. . . . The lovers, entirely absorbed in preparations for their departure, mingled feelings and itineraries, the past and the future, an inventory of the jewels and the organization of the relays of horses, reproaches and kisses. They already saw themselves out of reach, galloping along on the other side of the frontier, heedless of what they left behind—the scandal of their flight, the public reaction of a Hanover astounded by the disappearance of its Electoral Princess.

In July dawn breaks early. Knesebeck begged them to separate. Königsmark said: "Until this evening," and was gone like smoke with the astonishing moral and physical nimbleness that was typical of him. He was gay and full of hope. This was the lovely season and he was in the prime of his life. Everything would work out for the best.

He followed the corridor back the way he had come. He was about to open the door by which he had entered, but someone had bolted it.

There was another way out, the door of the Hall of the Knights which was not closed. Königsmark crept in noiselessly because he feared the vast, echoing emptiness. Scarcely had he entered than he received a violent blow on the head. The assassins had lept out from under the mantelpiece. Philipp Christoph threw himself back-ward. There is a historical controversy about whether he was armed. Some say he was not; others that he drew his sword and that it snapped (in any case, it was probably not one of those heavy battle swords with the blade widening at the hilt that are still known as königsmarks to armorers).

In the dawn's light the thugs recognized their victim as their chief. Immediately the Platen woman realized that the attack was weakening and she encouraged the assailants. Two soldiers had been wounded, but the others renewed the attack. Königsmark fell, run through by saber thrusts. His last words were those of a valiant warrior: "Spare the Princess; save the innocent Princess!" Leaning over him, the Platen woman closed his mouth with a kick of her heel.

Did she want him dead? Was she dreadfully distressed, as she pretended to be? It is said that she tried pouring a cordial between his lips, but that already he was no longer breathing. According to Palmblad, the Countess confessed her crime on her deathbed, and the minister who heard the confession mentioned it in the oration he gave at her funeral, which is written in his own hand and is said to be in the archives of Vienna.

Aghast, Madame Platen rushed to the Elector, who immediately began to reproach her with great violence: he had consented to an arrest, not a murder. Foreign courts would be up in arms because the victim was known throughout Europe. A frightful scandal would break out at dawn and Hanover would be covered with shame.

Daylight confronted them with the most urgent reality. Recovering his presence of mind, the Elector immediately took a course of action which might have seemed mad but which his rank and his authority were able to make plausible: to do away with the body and then deny everything. The story would be that Königsmark fled without leaving a trace, and after all, that could be the natural end of an adventurer in an age of continual peril, sudden absences and stays in far-off places. The Duke, as an absolute sovereign, was answerable to no one.

The Duke and his mistress hastened to the Hall of the Knights, where Königsmark's body lay on the floor. "The Elector kept his face hidden," says Pollnitz. "He was accompanied by an officer of the guards," writes the anonymous author of the *Mémoires du règne de Georges Ier*. Where to hide the body? It was impossible to go through the castle, for although everyone still slept, they would soon be awake. They could not reach one of the cellars or the park. But on the same floor there was a small room. They would pull up the floor, dig a hole, and fill it with quicklime.

When the sun rose, it was all over.

In the *Histoire secrette* it is related that one of the halberdiers, named Buschmann, who had taken part in the burial, later confessed to a priest named Cramer and told the whole story.

In his *Reminiscences* (1788), Horace Walpole asserts that Königsmark's remains were found during the reign of George II under Sophia Dorothea's dressing room, and that Königsmark had been strangled. Walpole claimed he had this from his father, Sir Robert Walpole, to whom the queen (Caroline of Anspach, the wife of George II and the daughter-in-law of Sophia Dorothea) disclosed it under the seal of secrecy at the beginning of the century. According to Thackeray (in *The Four Georges*) the body was burned on the day after the crime.

Sophia Dorothea did not go to bed. A brilliantly sunny July day dawned on a happiness so long awaited. That evening she would be free! She burned a great number of papers and made up a parcel of her jewels, which would enable her to subsist.[1] The lovers had discussed every-thing down to the smallest detail. The traveling coach would, for safety's sake, first take the road for Dresden, and once out of town would head for Wolfenbüttel.

Sophia Dorothea waited, counting the hours. A heavy silence, not of peace but of *in pace* hung over this old monastery converted into a residence.

There was nothing more to do but wait for Königs-mark's signal. . . .

At noon he had still given no sign of life.

It was Knesebeck who told her that Königsmark had not returned home, and that his servants were searching everywhere for him, and that they were most anxious for his life, especially as it was said that during the night there was a great commotion in one of the galleries of the palace and that a great deal of blood had been found on the spot, as though a man had been murdered.

Sophia Dorothea looked out the windows. On the banks of the Leine the passersby stopped, more of them every hour, and raised their heads as if to question the walls of the palace.

Despite her anguish, Sophia Dorothea had faith in her father-in-law. She valued his sensitivity, his culture, that respect for etiquette which would certainly prevent him from taking any brutal measures.

Sophia Dorothea tried to be patient. She would know more in the evening when her two children, George, a handsome little boy of eleven, and Sophia Dorothea, nine, would come as usual to wish her good night. . . . She waited for them in vain. Their absence tormented her. Had she been put in solitary confinement?

---

[1] *Mémoires de Sophie Dorothée* (London, 1845). See also Toland, *An Account . . .* (1709) and the *Letters* of Lady Mary Wortley Montagu.

Despite the thickness of the walls, rumors from the town began to filter through. It was said that Königsmark had been killed in a duel with a certain Count Lippe. In her panic Sophia Dorothea wanted to run to her father-in-law, but she was stopped. The Electress let it be known that she and Mlle. de Knesebeck were confined to their apartments.

7 / Aurora von Königsmark

Once the body had been covered with quicklime and walled up in a remote corner of the palace at Hanover, the Elector and Countess Platen breathed more easily. The matter was settled and there would be no more discussion about it. Who would worry about the disappearance of such an extravagant character as Königsmark? But a Königsmark could not be made to vanish as easily as his murderers. The Elector had not taken Aurora von Königsmark into consideration. She was a real nemesis, courageous and relentlessly tenacious.

Strange rumors began to circulate as early as the day after the murder. They reached Hamburg, where Aurora lived with the Löwenhaupts. All three began to worry, and their anxiety reached a peak with the arrival of Hildebrand, Königsmark's secretary. He brought with him a parcel given him by Mlle. de Knesebeck. Although under arrest and confined, she had succeeded in getting the parcel to him. It was sealed with Sophia Dorothea's coat of arms and on it was written: "To Countess Aurora von Königsmark, to be kept sealed until claimed by the hereditary Princess. If, however, it is not reclaimed, it is to be burnt without being opened and without its contents being read." The contents could only be the letters of Königsmark.

Deeply disturbed by Mlle. de Knesebeck's message, Hildebrand immediately went to his master's rooms, opened the wardrobes, trunks, bureaus, and hiding places of all kinds, and removed all the papers he had managed to find in the incredible disorder. He could not swear that he had not left behind anything compromising, because he had been interrupted by the arrival of commissioners charged by Madame Platen to make a search for her (doubtless to take not only the letters written by the Princess but those written by Platen too). Aurora added an unusual document to those Hildebrand brought. Palmblad, who tells the story, says the document had been given to her a few days before by the young accountant of a Hamburg banker with whom Königsmark had an account. Either from a sense of honor or because he wanted to revenge himself on his master, the accountant stole the document and brought it to Aurora. It was a letter written by Königsmark with his own inimitable spelling: Aurora could not doubt its authenticity. It announced to the Hamburg banker Lastrop that Königsmark was sending him the sum of 400,000 thalers and jewels worth 20,000 thalers. The banker was asked to keep this deposit after settling the debts which Count Philipp Christoph had contracted with him, and after putting 10,000 thalers at the disposal of Königsmark's sisters, should they have any financial problems. This paper, reproduced in full by Palmblad (who is the only author who mentions it) was not the least mysterious of this mysterious affair, because how could Königsmark have come into possession of this sum, which was enormous for the time and exceeded the liquid assets of most of the German princes? Did it come from Sophia Dorothea? But she herself was short of money, since she asked her father for some in order to flee from Hanover. Whatever the case, the banker denied ever having received the deposit and no trace of it was found.

Because the letter seemed authentic, the only reasonable hypothesis is that put forward by the banker: Königsmark entrusted this fortune to a messenger who either absconded with it or was robbed and perhaps murdered en route. Of greater value than this fabulous treasure were the trunks sent by Hildebrand after the sale of his master's house in Hanover. They contained 200 suits and uniforms, 47 fur-lined coats, 71 sabers, 102 watches, and 87 decorations. It was like so many relics of a great shipwreck, but for Aurora they were the relics of a beloved brother whom she wished to believe was still alive—kidnaped, imprisoned, but alive. She looked for him with passion, questioning everyone, knocking on all doors, writing to the Elector of Hanover, who kept silent, and to the Duke of Mecklenburg-Schwerin, who talked a lot but did very little. She turned up only vague rumors. Finally she decided to play her trump card: The Elector of Saxony.

The Holy Roman Empire of Germany was composed of more than six hundred states, from very large to tiny, from the Kingdom of Prussia with its millions of inhabitants to the Duchy of Oels Brandsfeld with its handful of subjects. In this "republic of princes," Ernst August held one of the most important positions.

Aurora was the most beautiful woman in Europe, the most learned, the most gifted, the one who could write the prettiest occasional verse. August the Strong had seen her at his mother's, the dowager Electress, on whom the Königsmark sisters called as they would on a distant relative. (The Königsmarks were related to several of the reigning families of Europe.) As soon as he saw Aurora again, in the full radiance of a beauty, a charm, and a quiet, proud dignity that were very rare at the court of Saxony, August fell in love with her and became most

164 ❦

indignant about the fate of her vanished brother. Urged on by Aurora, he made a threatening approach to Hanover, asking for his friend, his subject, his general— Königsmark. To pit Saxony against Hanover at a moment when Europe was committed to the Grand Alliance was a menacing maneuver which could bear on the outcome of the war and help Louis XIV. The Elector of Hanover grew frightened and intervened in Vienna. Had August of Saxony's persistence matched his enthusiasm, Aurora would have won, avenging her brother and influencing the destiny of Europe. But August the Strong was a weakling largely interested in conquering Aurora. In love as in politics, he was full of tricks. Palmblad relates that he promised nothing less than marriage once he had divorced his present wife. Aurora allowed herself to be duped by a sham marriage ceremony that had every appearance of being genuine. She was content but her Prince was infidelity personified. Women willingly submitted to him. To us he would seem like a Turk with his swarthy complexion and his enormous eyebrows, but he was admired in his time and his mistresses were legion: Countess Esserle, Princess Sobiesky, Madame de Spiegel, Princess Lubomirska, Madame de Hoyn, etc., etc. They became countesses of the Empire and their bastards were legitimized as chevaliers or even counts of Saxony.

Only Aurora's son, the little Maurice, who was the living image of August, remained fatherless. Abandoned by the Elector, Aurora remained alone in her palace where the walls were draped with "aurora silk."[1] She gave herself up entirely to melancholy reminiscences of her outings with the Elector in a gilded gondola on the

---

[1] *Aurore* in French means "golden yellow," among other things. — Trans.

Elbe River. . . . She never complained. With perfect tact and dignity she retired to the convent of Quedlinburg, of which she became abbess coadjutor and gave her son into the charge of Monsieur Delorme, a French tutor.

Quedlinburg had been founded eight hundred years before by Matilda, the beautiful wife of Emperor Henry the Fowler of the house of Saxony. She converted her widow's domain into an institution for young Catholic girls. For nearly nine centuries Quedlinburg defended its abbey and estates against the relentless avidity of neighboring princes. It took Napoleon to overpower it. The abbey fell into his hands through the treaty of Luneville and did not survive the destruction of the Holy Roman Empire. It was an essentially aristocratic order. All the nuns were princesses or at least countesses of the Empire—"canonesses of high distinction," as they were called. If Aurora never succeeded in becoming abbess, although it was promised to her at various times and she had the support of Prussia, it was not because her titles to nobility were in doubt, but because she excited the criticism and envy of the nuns by her glamour as a European celebrity, the distinguished visitors she received (including the Czarevitch, who was brought by the Duke of Wolfenbüttel), the receptions she gave, and the concerts in which she sang with her ever beautiful voice. Quedlinburg was anything but a cloister; witness the garden parties, the hunts, and other festivities celebrated there. But to the worthy nuns Aurora was always wrong; wrong to leave her little castle of Wilksen to visit her sister in Hamburg; wrong to bring lawsuits in Regensburg, Hanover, Bremen, and Stockholm for the restitution of her fortune. In 1698 she wanted to go as far as Poland to plead with King Charles XII in favor of the Königsmarks, who had been dispossessed by an unjust law. (Charles XII was in Poland at the time, having just defeated the Russians there against odds of three-to-one.)

August of Saxony, who had been elected King of Poland the year before and had taken up residence in Warsaw, was playing his habitual double game between the belligerents there. Löwenhaupt, who commanded a Saxon regiment, was very surprised to see his sister-in-law arrive in Warsaw not to reconquer the King's heart but to approach Charles XII. This did not stop August from visiting Aurora and, finding her as attractive as ever, from entrusting her with a diplomatic mission to the King of Sweden. Thus Aurora left for Mittau. She was the very picture of beauty and poetry, but Charles XII loved only war and was impervious to both her qualities. He refused to grant her an audience and when he passed on the road where she was waiting for him, he deigned only to doff his hat. Deeply hurt and angry, Aurora returned to Dresden, where she was surprised to learn that in a certain sense her mission had succeeded. The King of Saxony was pleased with her, and he was thinking of acknowledging the son whom she had borne him and who was destined one day to become the French Marshal de Saxe. But fate continued to harass the Königsmarks, raising them up only to cast them down even farther, and Aurora was not spared. She returned to Quedlinburg, where she passed years in obscurity, always waiting to be elected abbess and always disappointed at the last moment. She had to cope with all the princesses of the Holy Roman Empire who were without dowries or without husbands, and she was constantly called upon to pay her son's debts, then to support his abortive aspiration to the throne of Courland. For her son had inherited the adventurous character and basic absurdity of the Königsmarks, who always started as favorites and were always beaten at the post.

Toward the end Aurora suffered from dropsy and died during the night of February 15 to 16, 1728. Death did not bring peace to this stormy petrel. Her will disappeared together with what money she had. Her creditors descended on the remains and lawsuits raged. . . . In vain. There was not even enough left to pay for a decent burial. Like Königsmark and like Sophia Dorothea, Aurora has no tomb on which one may pray. When Palmblad[2] visited Quedlinburg he found only an old castle in ruins at the top of a hill. He asked to see Aurora's tomb; there was none. Among the tombstones of the princess-nuns, there was only a mummy of which the upper half remained. Palmblad leaned over the little yellowed face and thought he could still discern a trace of the charms which had been the glory and the misfortune of Aurora von Königsmark.

---

[2] Palmblad, *Aurora von Königsmark* (Leipzig, 1853).

8 / The Secret Dungeons of Ahlden 1694 – 1726

Meanwhile, in Hanover feelings mounted on the day after Königsmark's death. Ernst August was closely pursued by Banner, the envoy sent by the Elector of Saxony, who demanded more and more threateningly in his master's name that the "general of the Saxon cavalry, the Count of Königsmark," be returned to Saxony. Ernst August was terrified lest under pressure from August the Strong all the German princes who opposed Hanover should join against him. He temporized, he had the Emperor intervene, for the latter could not fail an ally who provided such good troops.

Hildebrand had not been able to remove all his master's papers, and the search ordered by Countess Platen turned up the letters of Sophia Dorothea. Von Metsch, the brother-in-law of Mlle. de Knesebeck and Königsmark's trusted friend, said that in Dresden he had seen Königsmark take great care of a parcel tied with a yellow ribbon and locked up in a box. Königsmark would have done better to burn these letters, which were Sophia Dorothea's undoing.

The Elector had them deciphered and read them with his mistress. He was livid. He would probably have forgiven the Königsmark adventure, for these cases of adultery hardly shocked him: after all, his own daughter. . . . But what was much more serious was the planned flight to Wolfenbüttel. The hereditary Electoral Princess was making ready to flee with her fortune to her cousin, the Elector's enemy; to flee into the camp of his irreconcilable neighbor! This was an act of high treason.

Locked in isolation in her apartments, Sophia Dorothea waited in anguish. She had had no news of Philipp Christoph. Eleonore de Knesebeck, locked up with her, knew nothing. Sophia Dorothea at last managed to send a clandestine call for help to her parents.

The *Histoire secrette* relates erroniously that the Duke of Celle was moved by the treatment his daughter was receiving and hastened to Hanover. "He criticized the scandal caused by the arrest of his daughter, but he soon changed his mind and approved everything that has been done. . . ."

In fact, the Elector had only had to send him the Count Platen, bearing the letters of Sophia Dorothea.

Contrary to what is stated in the apocryphal *Mémoires de Sophie Dorothée*, the letters contained entirely different sentiments than "gratitude to Königsmark, for having defended her interests." The *Histoire secrette* seems much closer to the truth: "Sophia Dorothea was told that Königsmark's papers had been seized; her plan to flee to France was revealed, as was her biting mockery of the Elector's affair with Countess Platen and her complaints about the harshness of her father, the Duke of Celle, and her husband, Prince George Louis. She described the former [the Duke] as an old tyrant and the latter [the Prince] as an executioner."

Where the Elector discerned a threat to the interests of Hanover, the Duke of Celle saw an offense to his family's reputation. The Duke's anger with his daughter only redoubled when his wife tried to defend her. We must not forget that at the time women were almost slaves. They were rarely consulted before being married off, their entire fortunes went to their husbands, and while men were allowed to be unfaithful, women's virtue was judged with great severity.

Although reading her daughter's letters shook Eléonore de Celle badly, she fell back on a last-ditch defense: if her daughter in an outburst of temper had shown herself unjust to her father, she had never committed adultery and she must be granted asylum.

The Duke was immovable: Sophia Dorothea was no longer his daughter. The couple had a confrontation as harrowing as that which had erupted when George Louis and Sophia Dorothea were engaged. Eléonore was twelve years older and she had lost all her influence over her intransigent husband. Henceforth political and family interests prevailed. To top it off, Eléonore asked the help and advice of the minister Bernstorff. Even after so many years she did not realize that he was an enemy, the creature of the Platen woman. Bernstorff only made matters worse. Eléonore tried one last time: "The Duchess of Celle threw herself at her husband's feet and begged him to protect the unfortunate Princess. He answered proudly that he no longer remembered having had a daughter."[1]

On his return to Hanover, Count Platen informed his master of the Duke of Celle's anger and of the success of his negotiation. Henceforth it would be possible to settle the future of the guilty Princess without opposition. One gets the feeling that the liaison had been known in Hanover for at least a year, and that action was only taken

---

[1] *Historie secrette*, p. 226.

when it became clear that Sophia Dorothea was about to flee, taking her fortune with her.

The Elector began by dispatching a messenger to Berlin to bring back George Louis, who was visiting his sister.

Then he sent his prime minister, Count Platen, to question Sophia Dorothea.

The Count expected to find a woman defeated, humiliated, crushed. He saw instead a very angry Princess imperiously demanding an explanation of the treatment to which she was being subjected.

"What is the meaning of this prison where I am being kept like a criminal?"

"His Most Serene Highness, the Elector, has deemed it reasonable to keep your Most Serene Highness under observation in case an . . . illegitimate . . . pregnancy. . . ."

Sophia Dorothea started:

"Do you take me for your wife?"

The Count did not turn a hair.

"The Elector has been aware of your relationship with Count von Königsmark."

"Where is Königsmark?" shouted Sophia. "Has he been locked up too?"

"I regret to announce to Your Highness that Count von Königsmark died two weeks ago."

Sophia Dorothea collapsed in a faint. Platen looked at her coldly without raising a hand to help her.

Sophia Dorothea came to:

"Murderers; they have murdered him! A family of murderers. . . ! Have pity and let me go! I can't stay here any longer. . . ."

"Your Most Serene Highness will be obeyed. She may leave at once if she wishes."

An officer of the guard entered to announce that the carriage was ready.

With the agreement of the Duke of Celle, who had given him full power to act as he thought best, the Elector Ernst August had made a rather wise decision. Sophia Dorothea's fate was difficult to decide for the moment. She could not be kept locked up at Leinenschloss without causing a scandal, and it would have been worse to allow her to go where she wished. So it was decided that she should leave Hanover as she desired, and be taken to the Duchy of Celle—not to her parents' palace, because the Duke refused to receive her, but to the little castle of Ahlden, where the local magistrate lived.

It was agreed that the name of Königsmark would never be mentioned and that her adultery would never be acknowledged. The Princess was leaving Hanover to live apart from Prince George Louis, "with whom she was no longer on good terms."

Eleonore de Knesebeck was made the scapegoat in this tragedy. She alone was guilty; she alone had poisoned the Princess' mind against her husband. As it was essential that Eleonore should not speak, she was put in prison.

Mad with grief and despair, fleeing like an animal that has lost its bearings far from its own forest, Sophia Dorothea threw herself into the carriage without knowing where they were taking her, solely to escape the horror of Leinenschloss. . . . Without seeing them, she passed through the forests of sad little birches, and by peat bogs flooded by the Aller that were interrupted by fields of cabbage that swarmed with mosquitoes.

When she finally saw her native land she heaved a sigh of relief. She was unaware that she was driving into a trap. The *Histoire secrette* ends with these awful words: "She arrived at the castle of Ahlden, six miles from Celle. The governor received her with much

respect . . . and announced to her that she was to remain
there for the rest of her days."

Naturally, this melodramatic statement is a fabrication. No one yet knew what Sophia Dorothea's fate
would be.

From the legal standpoint, Sophia Dorothea's silent
departure was insufficient grounds for divorce. But was
divorce the ultimate aim? For the Platen woman it surely was, and she worked to that end with all her cunning.
It is less certain that the Elector wanted a divorce.
Peace-loving, political, and easygoing, he would have
preferred a reconciliation. In his opinion, Sophia
Dorothea had every reason to stay in Hanover: a high
position, a royal future, her children. . . . He had not
understood that a cyclone had swept through this happy
scene, leaving a living corpse under the ruins.

Divorce proceedings took place in three stages, beginning with an attempt at reconciliation. Before Sophia
Dorothea was taken to Ahlden, a most curious scene took
place, if we are to believe Palmblad, who does not cite his
sources for the story:

"In Sophia Dorothea's drawing room a candlelit altar
was set up. In the presence of the high dignitaries of
Celle and Hanover [Palmblad names them] the priest
said a high mass. Then he solemnly called on the Princess to confess her sin if she was guilty and not to condemn herself to eternal punishment by swearing falsely.
Sophia Dorothea stated her innocence and took commun-
ion with such composure that she convinced those present. Thereupon the Elector offered his daughter-in-law
the chance to take her place again in the family home.
Everything would be forgiven and forgotten."

Thus the very real sin of adultery was erased. But who
worried about adultery in a court where it was apparently

more normal than fidelity? The accusation of adultery was the smoke screen behind which they wished to obscure the real, unpardonable, unforgettable crime of desertion and flight to Wolfenbüttel. It was this for which the Duke of Celle was unable to pardon his daughter until almost the end, and it was this which paralyzed even Duchess Eléonore's efforts to save her child.

The unlikely scene described by Palmblad was no doubt invented, but it does pose a problem. Was the adultery ever consummated that was so energetically, continuously, and angrily denied by Sophia Dorothea and Eleonore de Knesebeck? Did the lovers stop at the "embraces" they so much desired without going further (the danger of pregnancy would have been very great)? Was there an equivocal element which allowed the Princess and her faithful *confidente* to deny the adultery without perjuring themselves?

Would Sophia Dorothea have accepted her father-in-law's pardon if, as Palmblad asserts, the diabolical Bernstorff, posing as her official defender, had not dissuaded her? It is easier to imagine that, hardened by suffering and indifferent to all but the death of her lover, Sophia Dorothea could only think with horror of living in Hanover surrounded by Königsmark's murderers.

Sophia Dorothea had been at Ahlden since July 17 when she was unpleasantly surprised by a visit—not from her father or mother, as she expected—but from two ministers from the duchies of Celle and Hanover, Count von Bernstorff and Marshal de Bülow. For almost two hours these envoys tried to induce the Princess to agree in principle to a reconciliation.

You cannot save people despite themselves. Her prison

door had been opened, and she slammed it in the face of the envoys. She is even said to have declared: "If I am guilty of what I am accused of, I am not worthy of the Prince, and if I am innocent, it is he who is not worthy of me."

This statement is an obvious fabrication. Not once in the course of the lawsuit was Königsmark's name mentioned. It was feared "like a cholera epidemic."

The Electoral Princess thus having categorically and finally refused to return to the conjugal home and to her duties as a wife, the Electoral Prince sued for divorce.

The representatives of the Duke of Celle and those of the Elector conferred at Engesen. Celle asked for simple separation; Hanover wanted a divorce. Celle, as always, yielded in the end.

Earlier, in the hope of stopping the stir and the rumors in foreign courts, Hanover's representatives received and distributed a circular mentioning the disagreements between the Electoral Prince and his wife, and attributing them to the deceitful maneuvers of the lady in waiting, Eleonore de Knesebeck, who was alleged to have corrupted the Electoral Princess' mind.

Negotiations at Engesen were long and difficult. Sophia Dorothea's physical, moral, and material situation had to be settled down to the smallest detail. The agreement was signed on September 1, 1694. It consummated the complete ruin of the Princess, body and soul.

Soon thereafter Sophia Dorothea was taken to Lauenau. When she found herself once more in Hanoverian territory she was seized with terror. To reassure her, it was explained that her stay would only be temporary and that she was there to be closer to the court and, as soon as the divorce was made final, she would be freed again. She believed what she was told; she always believed everything.

The religious high court was established. It comprised eight members—four laymen and four churchmen, under the chairmanship of Privy Councillor de Busch.

These were fair-minded people who sought to respect their solemn oath of impartiality and justice. They quickly realized that everything had been settled in advance and that they were only there for form's sake; forms, at least, had to be respected. On several occasions they found fault with the proposed texts and had them changed. On each occasion Duchess Eléonore de Celle took advantage of the delay to try to protect her daughter. The judges wanted above all to be sure that no pressure was being brought to bear on the Princess to provoke the surprising speed with which she consented to everything. As a result they asked to hear her in person. This did not suit the Elector, who was most apprehensive about her violent language. Nonetheless, the judges had their way and Sophia Dorothea appeared. She was the despair of her lawyer, von Thiess, because of her inertia, her indifference, and her immediate affirmative answers. He tried in vain to make her understand how unjust was the clause forbidding her to remarry.

She was indifferent to everything provided that she left Hanover. She was like a child who only thinks about leaving the classroom. Even Königsmark had reproached her for this. "You must stop being a child," he once wrote.

Perhaps she thought that the divorce decree would set her completely free? The dukes were deceitful enough to leave her this illusion. She could not have suspected that she would be separated from her children forever and kept a prisoner until her death.

Who could have told her this? None of the judges knew the intentions of the two dukes. Von Thiess did everything to caution the Princess not against the prison, which awaited her, but against the clause that forbid her, the guilty spouse, from remarrying while George Louis, the innocent spouse, was free to remarry. This clause also infuriated the Duchess of Celle. She fought for a long time and almost overcame the obstinacy of her husband, but he was only putty in the hands of his brother. And, of all the solutions, the one the Elector feared most was the possibility of a remarriage which would have taken Sophia Dorothea out of Hanover, along with her present fortune and future inheritance. Eléonore d'Olbreuse alone fought for her daughter with admirable energy and tenacity, and for a time she even succeeded in getting Bernstorff to work for her. The clause forbidding remarriage was very nearly struck out, but the Elector insisted on it above all others, just as he insisted on the prison, for he dreaded a change of heart on the part of the Duke of Celle, which would lead him to pardon his daughter and restore her property.

For the same reason the Elector did not want to part with Sophia Dorothea's letters, which the Duke of Celle wanted to see burned in the presence of the councillors. The Duke insisted in vain; and the Elector kept the letters. Did he intend to use them to refresh his brother's memory should the Duke's resentment weaken? Despite everything, one may well wonder whether Sophia Dorothea's lot might not ultimately have been improved by the man who appeared to be her worst enemy, Ernst August, her father-in-law. He was sensitive and humane; he loved his daughter-in-law and was concerned about her. It was not in his character to hold a grudge forever. Certainly, Hanover came before everything else for him, but he would have understood this young creature's awful fate and would no doubt have allowed her to see her children again and receive her friends.

He was not narrow-minded, stupid, and obstinate, like the Duke of Celle. But Sophia Dorothea was dogged by fate: the events of this somber year dealt the Elector's health a blow from which he did not recover. He lingered on for four years and died after sending a messenger to Celle, asking his brother to swear never to change the arrangements he had made with regard to George Louis.

The court's verdict was rendered on December 28. It summed up in a few lines the Princess' refusal to return to her husband and declared in consequence "the ties of matrimony dissolved and a second marriage forbidden." The Princess was notified of this verdict on December 31, in her residence at the magistrate's house. She expected to leave at once for Ahlden, but here again promises were broken. It is said that she spent nearly a year at Lauenau . . . before once again crossing the drawbridge of Ahlden.

Ahlden was more a fortress than a castle. Almost all of it remains intact today.

The date over the façade is 1579. The drawbridge to the old stronghold, called the Magistrate's House, has disappeared, and the moats on the north side have been replaced by a paved avenue lined with old lime trees. A roof of mossy tiles rests on brick walls that are broken by black half-timbering in the shape of St. Andrew's crosses. The castle is oriented toward the south, giving on the Aller River, which forms a natural moat before flowing on to Verden and its confluence with the Weser. The castle has remained standing for centuries, but it is falling into ruins. Its little courtyard is scarcely larger than a farmyard and its service buildings could scarcely have held a troop of guards. One wonders where the forty soldiers of the escort lived, not to mention the Princess' suite and the spies planted among the servants by Madame Platen. The gravelly land, which is a terminal moraine, has preserved something of the Quaternary period, something moldy and perpetually damp—a mud on which a Nordic civilization was laid down, for this land long belonged to Sweden. The black earth, once flooded, adds to the sad appearance of the place. A few fields of puny buckwheat are scattered through the pale pink heather. Although it is quite close to both Verden and Bremen, nothing at Ahlden evokes memories of those cities—of the Hanseatic League, of the masts of ocean-going sailing ships rising among the gables of the city halls and cathedral spires, of the riches of the Far East in the burghers' houses, those riches that left their mark in delft porcelain and in the *chinoiserie* decorations of gilded wooden consoles. At Ahlden we are in the heart of some Scandinavian dungeon. The horizon itself seems barred by slender pines, their trunks straight and leafless. The landscape is indescribably ugly and sad, formless and colorless. As far as the eye can see there are expanses of gray water and gray grass under a gray sky. For thirty years this is all that the "innocent princess" saw with her velvety eyes from her rust-colored prison.

Did Sophia Dorothea think back when she entered this tomb? Did she consider that if she had been shrewder she would have kept up appearances, refused to write those madly imprudent letters, and rejected all idea of flight? Did it occur to her that she had ceaselessly played into the hands of her enemies, allowing the house of Hanover to get rid of her without even needing to mention Königsmark's name?

Happily for us who love her, she could not have had any such thoughts. That warm, generous nature was indifferent to self-interest and to ambition. She thought only of giving herself entirely. Like Catherine de Heilbronn of Kleist, who threw herself from a window to follow her knight without reflecting that the air would not hold her up, and thus broke both legs, Sophia Dorothea of Celle ruined her life to follow her lover.

Scarcely had the Princess arrived at Ahlden than incredibly severe orders were given to Monsieur de la Fortière, Grand Falconer of the court of Celle and the governor of the castle, to keep the secret inviolate. One would think they came not from a father but from the most implacable of judges: the hereditary Electoral Princess was not to communicate with the outside world . . . any infraction of these rules would be punished by death . . . everyone entering or leaving the castle would be searched . . . the Duchess of Celle herself was not to have the right to see or write to her daughter!

The Elector controlled Sophia Dorothea's income and allowed her a pension of 8,000 thalers a year—the equivalent of $2,880. This sum would be increased to $4,320 on the death of the Duke of Celle and to $5,280 when the Princess reached forty years of age. It was a very comfortable sum for the time. The little duchy of Ahlden was her property and henceforth she was to be called the Duchess of Ahlden. Her real name was expunged from the registers in Hanover and from all official documents. It also disappeared from church prayers.

Formerly Königsmark's letters were cautiously headed: "To the known person." Now Sophia Dorothea had become the unknown person.

Unknown . . . but not by everyone. It was impossible to keep tongues from wagging in the European courts. Königsmark was too famous, and too many people were still concerned about his fate. Until the end of the eighteenth century he was sought everywhere. His fate aroused interest in Dresden, Vienna, The Hague, Berlin, Stockholm, Copenhagen. The official circulars from Hanover and Celle were most inadequate for maintaining appearances. Ministers residing there wrote about the event in their dispatches, of which the most curious was from Stepney, the British envoy to Dresden. His letter of July 24, 1694, written shortly after the murder, must have escaped the official *autodafé* of George I's time. It betrays the macabre humor of the classic British diplomat. The dispatch was addressed to Cresset, his colleague in Hanover:

I am very curious to know what piece of mischief has been brewing in Hanover. If you do not trust the post where you reside, let me know in cipher, and give me all the details on the Hereditary Princess' ruin. Amours are fatal in your parts; we have had a foretaste of this here. But at present the Tragedy has moved to your Court, and I fear daggers and poison will be as familiar among you as they are in Italy. Your Princes have been often there, and may have learned the humor of the country of dispatching people without noise. A servant or two of Count Königsmark's have run frequently between this place and Hanover, as I have heard Count Berlo's dog did between the Camp and Brussels after the battle of Fleurus, seeking out his master, from whom he had no news. Our Elector sent one of his Adjudants, to stop the blow if it was not yet given. But I suppose the corpse, by this time, is in the common shore, and your

Elector, by a fortunate coincidence, has cleared the debt of 30,000 thalers that my Elector owed the deceased for two years. I have been told that his two sisters rave like Cassandra, and want to know what happened to their brother; but in Hanover they answer (like Cain about his brother) that they are not their brother's keeper, and that if the body should be found, the murder will be left as much in the dark. . . . I knew him (Königsmark) in England, in Hamburg, in Flanders, and in Hanover for a dissolute debauchee, whom I would always have avoided. . . . He is not to be regretted. . . .[2]

At Versailles too the romance of Königsmark and Sophia Dorothea was passionately discussed. Louis XIV himself, while at table, deigned to question his sister-in-law, the Princess Palatine, about the affair, and it is not difficult to imagine the answers. "This miserable creature deserved her misfortune" was doubtless her theme, for the Princess, like the Electress, was implacable in her hate and contempt and never forgave this d'Olbreuse "misalliance," which forever prevented the British royal family from being accepted as truly blue-blooded in Germany (A. W. Ward). This French woman, who would barely have been a worthy match for the valet of "Monsieur" the King's brother, had had the unheard of audacity to crash the oldest aristocracy in the world! The letters that the Princess Palatine wrote to her aunt, the Electress Sophia, at the time of the tragedy were naturally burned, but she wrote others. For example, on April 29, 1702, she wrote to Countess Louise: "The Duchess of Celle has more reasons than anyone to lament her daughter's misfortune, because if she had not brought

---

[2] Quoted in W. H. Wilkins, Vol. II.

her up in her earliest youth for coquetry and gallantry, she would never have been plunged into misfortune. There are people here to affirm that she did not behave criminally at all; but a young woman like her who allows herself to be embraced and caressed does everything else too."

The Princess Palatine was certainly right about one thing: Sophia Dorothea had been brought up by her mother not, indeed, to be coquette, but as a young French aristocrat both sensitive and proud. Had she been brought up the daughter of a German sovereign, she would have been fascinated at the prospect of the crown of England and would have been delighted to marry George Louis. After all, it has taken two world wars and several revolutions to kill the ideal rooted in the heart of every princess of the blood of becoming a queen.

Meanwhile at Hanover, plays and balls were staged so that Sophia Dorothea would be forgotten. The effort was not always successful because if no one at court dared pronounce her name, the common people missed and bewailed their Princess. There were demonstrations and petitions which terrified the Elector and above all the Platen woman. For what would happen if the Duke of Celle's resolve was shaken and he gave his daughter her liberty? The Elector feared such a change of heart until his death. This worry, and perhaps also a certain remorse, affected his health. He had his first warning of this, and yet the festivities continued despite the family crisis. "Very provoking," wrote the British envoy Cresset, scandalized. Above all there was a famous banquet, commemorating Trimalchio's,[3] that was described in incredible detail by the philosopher Leibnitz in a letter

---

[3] Trimalchio, a vulgar upstart, was the hero of the *Satyricon*, written during the first century probably by Petronius Arbiter. Of the fragments that have survived, the most complete describes "Trimalchio's Banquet."

to the Princess Hohenzollern. He said there were as many beds as there were guests. Although in Rome it was the custom to put two or three people in the same bed, in Hanover people liked their creature comforts.[4] "The queen [of Prussia] and their Highnesses The Elector and the Duke Ernst August took part; but the Electress and his Highness the Duke of Celle only came to watch." Trimalchio's spoils of war were empty bottles. . . . As the guests entered a slave shouted: "Right foot forward. . . !" The banquet took place in the great hall that was longer than it was wide. In the middle were nine elaborate ceremonial serving dishes, but the dishes containing things to eat were laid out on either side, nearer the guests. . . . In the center was a dish full of live fish with two satyrs pouring water over them as if it were bouillon to serve as a sauce. On either side were straw-filled baskets in which a hen was laying eggs. . . . Beyond the baskets was a donkey carrying two sacks of salad and olives; then a hare, larded and roasted, winged as though it were Pegasus. . . . Next to the donkey was a pie that concealed live birds. . . . As Trimalchio entered he was preceded by a huntsman and followed by eight pages dressed as slaves with candles in their hands and trumpets and drums. . . . Trimalchio was lowered onto his bed and begged his guests' pardon for having made them wait, saying that he had been in the bath. Then he invited the company to rejoice, for it was the day on which his young lover was shaved for the first time—an occasion that the ancients celebrated with some ceremony. "Let us drink Falerno wine," he said [this was the name he gave to the good wine of Tokay]. "Why should we not drink some since it lasts longer than we do?"

---

[4] Malortie, *Der Hannoversche Hof*, 1847, pp. 162ff.

Sophia Dorothea did not hear about these brilliant carnivals. The silence around her was never interrupted by music, laughter, or the sound of a friend's voice. She heard only the footsteps of her pages; the conventionally respectful words of the marshals of the court who served her in turn, doing their job as spies; the exhortations of her chaplain, pastor C.; or the chattering of the storks. . . . Her carriage, surrounded by mounted guards, could only take her six miles from Ahlden toward Hayden, as far as a bridge which she was forbidden to cross. On foot she was only allowed onto the ramparts between two guards. Not until the summer of 1695 was she allowed out of doors because she really suffered from the heat and there were fears for her health. This was something that George Louis worried about, for he remembered the prediction that he would die in the same year as his wife. With incredible cruelty the Hanoverian princes, and even her own father, had denied her all visits and all correspondence. Eléonore had to wait for four years for the permission to see and write her daughter. What was Sophia Dorothea's life like during those four mortal years? What were her thoughts?

When she had recovered somewhat from her terrible despair, her hate, her need to flee, she began to write. In her journal she tirelessly wrote the story of her misfortune—the story that was the ancestor of all the apocryphal accounts that were to follow. She also wrote memoranda for her legal defense, poems, and letters—to her father begging him to forgive her, to the Electress Sophia expressing her condolences on the death of the Elector, and letters pleading that she be allowed to see her children. There was never a reply. It appears that toward the end of his life the Duke of Celle wanted to see his daughter again, but the wily Bernstorff always dissuaded him. However, on one occasion the Duke did not listen to his minister and arranged to go to Ahlden the day after the hunt. He died during the night, and his passing was a horrible blow to Sophia Dorothea. She lost her only protector (if he can be called that), and the Duchy of Celle became the property of her hated husband, George Louis, already Elector because of the death of his father.

The Duke of Celle died in 1705, designating Sophia Dorothea his unique heir but reaffirming the principle of her lifelong imprisonment. By a strange perversity of fate, this recluse who lived alone with a ghost, grew richer. The money, which would have allowed her to flee with Philipp Christoph, arrived too late.

The world that Sophia Dorothea had known had changed. . . . She herself had become something like a defeated nation that has been forced to sign an unconditional surrender. In the lethargy of extreme grief she sat by her window watching the Aller flow by and the seasons succeed one another. She no longer had the strength to surface again. During the foggy nights at Ahlden the vision of Königsmark haunted her. She prayed a great deal and fulfilled her religious duties to the letter, but he filled her dreams. She imagined herself riding with Königsmark again at Celle, she on her Hanoverian horse whose mane was braided in the shape of a bow and decorated with the ducal colors, and he looking magnificent in his deerskin jerkin. She saw herself again dancing the polonaise with him to the music of Bach, holding his hand during the promenade around the dinner table. . . . She continued to dress up for this dear ghost. The frivolous spirit of fashion floats above storms. The imprisoned Princess had seen the passing in turn of farthingales and trains, and soon she would wear the first petticoats with hoops of whale-bone. Her enemies said that she lived in front of her mirror. In the evening she dressed for the memory of her lover. It was an extraordinary spectacle to see this woman alone in the little dining room at Ahlden (a whitewashed cell that still exists). The high black bow of ribbon in her coiffure would be arranged in rays and covered with precious stones that glinted under a Venetian lace scarf, and she would arrange around her arm-chair a dress of black moire with wide flounces, russet pleats, and gold braid. She was a prisoner dressed not in sackcloth but in silk, and chained with diamonds. Her first lady in waiting would present the napkin, the second would taste the meats, and many lackeys would serve her under the glass eyes of a stuffed bear (for how could she not remember the bear that Königsmark had trained to tear out his heart if the Princess ever left him?).

"She is not at all to be pitied," the implacable Palatine wrote again and again. And in fact the dreadful thing was not the way Sophia Dorothea was treated but the despair she felt when she realized that what she thought was her homeland, having passed into her husband's hands, had become the property of her worst enemy and her prison for life.

While her father was still alive, she had tried to appease him and to move him by her obedience. Little by little she had developed the habit of obeying until all her powers of resistance were gone. One day when a fire broke out at Ahlden, Sophia Dorothea remained motionless in the corridor, her jewel box under her arm, exposed to the flames and refusing to move without an order from the governor. This incident, related by Wilkins, shows how her spirit had been broken once and for all.

In April 1700, French troops advanced to Ahlfeld, quite close to Ahlden (probably as part of the campaign at the beginning of the century against the Barrier towns[5]). Sophia Dorothea was ordered to move to Celle, and she was overjoyed to return to the castle and the apartments where she had lived as a girl. She stayed for nearly a year amid the sympathy of the common people. Why did she not profit by her stay to escape? Wolfenbüttel was quite close. . . . Was it because she was watched or because she was in despair? One must believe the latter, for she was a broken woman.

Letters from the Princess Palatine, dated August 1700, relate that once the danger had passed, Hanover insisted more and more heatedly that Sophia Dorothea should return to Ahlden. She was obliged to do so despite the efforts of her mother. But even this did not end the Princess Palatine's hostility for, as late as 1702, she wrote to her aunt: "The Duchess of Ahlden has been seeing her mother." According to the *Mémoires de Sophia Dorothée*, from 1717 to 1720 mother and daughter saw each other often. The Princess Palatine's letters continued until 1712, when the Electress Sophia died, and the tone was always the same: "She is not to be pitied all that much."

Sophia Dorothea was like the corpse of one of those adulteresses that the sultans would order thrown into the Bosporus: when the water closed over the sack containing the body, small boats and gondolas would again crisscross the surface to the sound of music.

Sophia Dorothea felt only one thing: horror at her

---

[5] The Barrier Treaties, signed in 1709 and 1715, brought several towns (Villes de la Barrière) together under the jurisdiction of the States General of the Spanish Netherlands. The aim was to protect Holland from the French with this buffer zone. — Trans.

husband, nothing more. Her position as a princess had accustomed her to keep silent and wait; an adorable creature had brought her out of this passivity. He was the first and would be the last; he was no more, so she was no more.

The death of the Duke of Celle was a misfortune for the Duchess Eléonore too. Until the end he had been anxious to make her future secure, and indeed he left her extremely well provided for. But she had nothing but loathing for her son-in-law, George Louis, who had become the master of Celle. The *Histoire secrette* confirms it: "This death brought about a great change in the fortunes of the Duchess Eléonore. Her son-in-law, who became the sovereign of Celle, let himself be ruled completely by Count von Bernstorff, who took the place of Count Platen. Count Platen had died after being blind for the last six years of his life. Bernstorff never stopped causing the Duchess grief and she had great difficulty maintaining continued access to her daughter. Duchess Eléonore was obliged to leave the palace at Celle although George Louis never came to occupy it, and she endured all sorts of outrages."

The Duchess of Celle died in 1722, having been reduced to the level from which she had raised herself little by little with such difficulty and effort until she reached the rank she had never dared hope for. Sophia Dorothea lost her only consolation, for her mother had eventually managed to write her, visit her, and bring her news of the outside world. Sophia Dorothea inherited the domain of Olbreuse, which Louis XIV had returned to the Duchess of Celle in 1707. She also inherited the domain of Wienhausen, other lands, her mother's jewels and furniture, and 60,000 thalers deposited in Holland.

And what good was it all? The prisoner of Ahlden was irrevocably and forever alone.

She knew of her dear Knesebeck only that she had been imprisoned for a long time in the fortress of Springe, where she was in solitary confinement. She was treated this way because all the blame had been thrown on her and she had to be prevented from talking. She was nicknamed the "lady in disgrace."[6] Later she had been transferred to the fortress of Schwarzfels, where perhaps she might have spent the rest of her days. . . . She too wrote a great deal, even with charcoal on the walls of her cell. But she had friends and she escaped. The prison roof being in need of repairs, one of her friends disguised himself as a roofer, made a hole through the tiles and then through the ceiling. He managed to lower a rope into the cell and haul Eleonore de Knesebeck up onto the roof. "Eluding her guards," the *Histoire secrette* says, "she fled after having had the courage to slide down from a height of 180 feet." The *confidente* found asylum at Wolfenbüttel, to the consternation of the court at Hanover, which deemed it necessary to reinforce the surveillance at Ahlden. It is argued that Mlle. de Knesebeck probably did confide in her protector. Of more interest is the fact that Sophia Dorothea's daughter, when she became Queen of Prussia, summoned Eleonore de Knesebeck to her court. A faint ray of hope shone through the dark windows of Ahlden.

Sophia Dorothea had failed to receive help from her mother during her divorce and at the beginning of her long martyrdom. Might this help not come from her children? The elder, George, was now about twenty,

---

[6] *Demoiselle de deshonneur*, in French, a play on the phrase *demoiselle d'honneur*, lady in waiting. — Trans.

and her daughter, and namesake, Sophia Dorothea, was fifteen. It is more than likely that they both loved and missed their mother, that they tried to see her again, that they thought of her, and that they detested their father. It is difficult to understand their lack of success. Perhaps after so many centuries we are not sufficiently aware of the pressures of heredity, politics, and society on these children of ruling houses. Eléonore did her best to see that they should not forget their mother, and nature helped. The children resembled their mother physically and by temperament, particularly the Prince; he had her vivacity, her bright hazel eyes, her brown hair.

The story is often told of how the young Prince, out hunting one day, left his retinue and galloped toward Ahlden. His companions pursued him and managed to catch up with him just as his mother, having caught sight of him from a window, was beckoning him. The governor refused to admit the Prince to the castle, and on his return the boy was severely reprimanded. Much later the future King George II would show other signs of attachment to the memory of his mother. Like her mother, the daughter was very beautiful and in 1706 she married for love, Frederick Wilhelm I, later King of Prussia. After a rather long while she began to write secretly to her mother. "The mother pleaded for help; her daughter promised to help her recover her liberty . . . her husband, the King of Prussia, did not dare oppose her for his own sake."[7]

By inheriting from her father, and later from her mother, the Duchess of Ahlden became the richest princess in Europe. A hundredth part of this fortune

---

[7] Wilkins, Vol. II., p. 635.

would have allowed Sophia Dorothea to flee to happiness with Philipp Christoph, yet by a dreadful stroke of irony it had come too late. Worse than useless, it was harmful, because it only strengthened the bonds around the prisoner. The money, the estates, the jewels excited everyone's greed: her husband, family, servants, and ministers all kept a wary eye on the treasure. Out of self-interest her son-in-law, Frederick Wilhelm, the first King of Prussia, allowed his Queen to correspond with her mother, the Duchess of Ahlden. The letters aroused in the prisoner a burning urge to be free. She dreamed of escape and galloped madly along the six miles of road which were open to her "with a rage similar to the rage of Napoleon at St. Helena," commented Ward somewhat inappropriately.

The very strength of the dream allowed this gentle creature, as incapable of foresight as of prudence, to accumulate in a Dutch bank a capital of 300,000 thalers from the dowager Duchess of Celle, plus her own accumulated income. To prepare her escape she needed a clever and devoted agent. The Queen of Prussia recommended Count von Bahr, but then, having received unfavorable reports, she urged her to be suspicious. However, Sophia Dorothea was incapable of harboring suspicions: she was always betrayed, she was born to be betrayed—by her father, her brother-in-law, her husband, and above all by her lover, whose ferocious, mad jealousy had brought her to ruin. So despite the warnings of her daughter, who had seen through him, Sophia Dorothea continued to trust her adviser, von Bahr. For years she believed in him: he was her last, her only hope. She put all the money she had in Holland in his name . . . and the miserable wretch stole it.

This final revelation of human villany killed Sophia

Dorothea. She wrote a few words, which she gave to a messenger, and collapsed. Was it a stroke or meningitis? She suffered frightfully: she screamed, refusing the doctors, surgeons, and chemists whom George I, terrified, sent to Ahlden. It was impossible to save her. Those around her could only tremble as they heard the terrible curses, the appeals of the prisoner for divine justice against the cruel tyrant who had made himself her jailer and who had stolen thirty years of her life.

She died on November 13, 1726, aged sixty, after being a prisoner for thirty-two years.

9 / Monument to Sophia Dorothea

After 1694, time stood still for Sophia Dorothea at Ahlden. But for the Elector in Hanover, it marched on ever more quickly.

His Serene Highness George Louis, Elector of Hanover, was there in all his majesty, his fat, his laziness, his honors, and his habits, never having read a book; never having considered a single problem. He was awash in thalers, income, and inheritances.

Melville, his admirer, makes him out to be an honest, sensible man, just, prudent, and fair, without desires or ambitions.

If he were all that, how could he have lived barely fifty miles from the unfortunate prisoner without thinking even for a moment of forgiveness? How could he forbid her to see or write to her children? Was not this just man ashamed? Did this honest man have no scruples? Can his behavior be explained uniquely by self-interest, taking into account that a first effect of a kinder attitude would have involved restoring his wife's property? Or was it because he feared a past not entirely buried with Königsmark's corpse? Was the root cause hate or vengeance?

This had gone on for nearly twenty years.

Gradually, without effort on his part, and almost without his knowledge, George Louis was carried upward on the wings of success. With every passing year he became an increasingly important personality, and Hanover a more powerful state. By this time his warring days had passed, and he no longer led those swift, distant, and dangerous campaigns in which he clashed swords from Hungary to Greece, from Denmark to Flanders.

Since Sophia Dorothea had left his life, fortune smiled on him.

He became Elector on the death of his father in 1698, thereby effortlessly profiting by all the dogged efforts Ernst August had exerted to attain the Electorate. It had taken him ten years to force the doors of the College. George Louis was now Arch Treasurer of the Empire.

When his father-in-law died in 1705, George Louis united Celle with Hanover. He did not deign to live there, and instead was represented in Celle by a Regency Council.

In 1700, as the father-in-law of the King of Prussia, he had signed a treaty of alliance with that power. Since then Hanover had become a powerful fortress, flanked as it was by the Prussian bastion on one side and by the Dutch stadholder in the west.

When Willem of Orange had become King of England, and the Dutch were seeking a stadholder, it was of George Louis that they thought.

In 1706 the Emperor named George Louis Imperial Commander of the forces of the lower Rhine during the Grand Coalition against Louis XIV. In 1711 he resigned the post, for he did not get on with Marlborough or with Prince Eugene, and persisted in treating them as equals.

In the same year he delegated a plenipotentiary to the negotiations that began in Utrecht, just as the Emperor and the King of England did.

Secure in his palace of Herrenhausen, he feared no one. He installed his mistress there and relegated his mother, the Electress Sophia, to a distant wing of the chateau. He never ceased to improve and decorate this palace with antiques and orange trees from Italy, paintings from Holland, curios from the Far East, and a troupe of French actors. His stables housed 600 horses[1] and 30 court coaches. According to Toland, His Serene Highness had an income of 3,000 thalers; according to Pollnitz, he left 6 million crowns when he died. The silver mines in the Harz Mountains and the sale of soldiers brought in more than ever. To crown this mass of honors, promotions, and material advantages, the Act of Succession voted by the British Parliament suddenly made obvious the role that Hanover might one day be called on to play, although at the time the chances that George Louis might succeed to the British throne were very remote, given the fifty-seven Stuarts who took precedence over him. Moreover, the throne of England did not interest the Elector; he was too fond of his comforts and of Germany.

This was not his mother's point of view. Although she was kept away from the affairs of state, and despite her eighty-four years, she was ambitious, farsighted, and lived intensely. While used to the deviousness and patience required in politics, she remained vigorous, passionate, arrogant, and inflexible by nature. As more and more Stuarts died off around Queen Anne, Princess Sophia looked to the future.

In 1700, Queen Anne's sole surviving son, the Duke of Gloucester, died of smallpox, marking the end of the direct line of the Stuart succession.

---

[1] "The Cavalry School of Hanover is the direct descendant of the Versailles School" (James Fillis).

The first in line was now the Duchess of Savoy, the daughter of Henrietta of England. However, the Duke of Savoy had ceased to support the Orange camp, and had thus fallen out with England. Following the deaths, conversions to Catholicism barred the route to the throne to a number of pretenders in the line of succession. Eleven sovereign houses were in line: Savoy, Orleans, Lorraine, Bourbon, Modena, Austria, Prussia, etc. Hanover would win. The elder German branch, the Wolfenbüttels, might have competed, but Sophia Dorothea's only friend, the Duke was converted to Catholicism in 1710. In the Electress Sophia's own family, everyone—mother, sisters, and nieces—had become Catholic. With each conversion, the house of Hanover's claim became stronger. Sophia, who was a cousin of the Stuarts and a passionate Anglophile, now declared: "It matters little when I die as long as my tomb is inscribed with the words: 'Queen of England and Ireland.'"[2]

Before the reign of Queen Anne, the Stadholder of Holland (later William III of England), who was a lukewarm supporter of Hanover, suggested to King James II that the Stuart Prince of Wales be considered, brought to England, and induced to convert to Anglicanism if only for form's sake. But the exiled king refused.

Little by little the chances of the House of Hanover improved. After the Act of Succession (1689), the English Parliament voted the Act of Settlement (1701). George Louis received the Order of the Garter. In 1702 Sophia's name appeared in the *Book of Anglican Prayer*. The crisis was accentuated when Louis XIV recognized James III.

There were already two kings of France, since the kings

---

[2] *Mémoires du règne de George 1er*, Anonymous (The Hague, 1729).

of England for centuries had called themselves kings of France. When Louis XIV recognized the Stuart pretender, there were also two kings of England and, of course, two princes of Wales.

The English Parliament then adopted the Bill of Naturalization, and then the Act of Regency. George Louis was made Duke of Cambridge. Finally, in 1712, an English law gave Sophia and her son precedence over all other British subjects.

It would be an oversimplification to suggest that Queen Anne had decided to have the House of Hanover succeed her. The last seven years of her reign were full of intrigues between Hanoverians and Jacobites, between Whigs and Tories. These were made the more complex by the fact that certain Whigs supported the Pretender while some Tories favored the Hanoverian. The Electress Sophia showed her sympathy for the Whigs while in her heart remaining attached to the direct line of the Stuarts. Through her letters she multiplied her contacts with the Court of St. James, and hypocritically mourned the son of James II, "the poor Prince of Wales." When lords Halifax and Dorset came to Hanover to present her with the Bill of Naturalization, she received them with great pomp and ceremony. Then, suddenly, she rushed to the far end of the drawing room and turned to the wall the portrait of the Jacobite pretender, which had not been taken down. (There is a real art to knowing when to remove certain portraits.)

These intrigues appeared to leave George Louis indifferent. When he had been sounded out from London about whether he would renounce Hanover in case he should be called to reign in England, he had said he would not. But by a curious quirk of fate everything that ought to have kept him from the throne, including his character, brought him closer to it. He did not fail, and would never fail to let the English know that if he became their king it would be because he was obliged to, and that he really preferred his Hanover. His English supporters explained to him the need for propaganda, but he refused to subsidize the pamphleteers or pay the debts of needy members of the House of Lords, such as Sunderland. Because they wanted him to be represented in the increasingly likely event of the Queen's death, the Whigs insisted that he send his son to England. But George Louis refused.

Queen Anne was weak, sick, and irresolute. Except for the Scottish troops, most of her army was favorable to the Hanoverians. Her kingdom was on the verge of civil war, and she backed both sides while continuing in her heart to favor the Pretender, "the King over the water." But she followed the advice of Bishop Wilkins who, as a good Anglican, told her: "If Your Majesty opts for the Pretender, She will be locked up in the Tower within a month and dead three months later." Anne was annoyed when she was left to one side and displeased when she thought people were trying to force her hand. Despite her shrewdness, the Electress Sophia could not make head or tail of the situation. More and more exasperated, she ostentatiously refused to go to England, and set the Queen against her by her maneuvering. Although the Queen called her "madam, sister, and aunt" in her famous letter of March 19, 1714, she put the Electress in her place. This letter was followed by one to George Louis with the identical message: Do not upset my subjects by your intrigues and do not darken the end of my reign with undue agitation. Sophia, terrified, thought she could read her own condemnation between the lines.

Sophia was taking too much exercise. She exhausted all who accompanied her on her walks along the paths at Herrenhausen. Although she had replied to Anne's letter most deferentially, which should have set her conscience at rest, the tacit threat contained in the Queen's letter was a fatal blow to her. Those around her tried to keep the octogenarian Electress in good health by saying: "Your Highness should not walk too fast." "That is true," she replied, and then fell to the ground, struck down by apoplexy.

If she had lived two months longer, her dream would have been realized and she would have seen her son become King of England.

This remarkable woman inspired respect, esteem, and admiration, but never either sympathy or pity. Her harshness toward Sophia Dorothea was unforgivable. She was a mother and knew the sufferings of a mother, since the death of her three sons almost killed her. Yet scornful silence was her only answer to the desperate appeals of the prisoner of Ahlden that she be allowed to see her children. Sophia herself was utterly virtuous: Why then did she blithely indulge the many affairs of her daughter, the Electress of Brandenburg, while showing a pitiless severity toward Sophia Dorothea's only great love? The Electress Sophia, the outraged and irreproachable wife, pushed respect for the conventions so far that she assumed the defense of her husband's insolent mistress when she wrote: "Countess Platen is not accustomed to being spoken of in the manner adopted by the 'Orrors' [Aurora von Königsmark]." Harshness was the mark of her character. Of her brother-in-law, to whom after the threadbare Duchy of Osnabrück, she owed her fine palace in Hanover and her magnificent collections, she wrote: "He died as a good German, glass in hand." And of her son George Louis she spoke in terms so scathing that none of the critics of the future king could have outdone her.

In causing the Electress Sophia to die in a paroxysm of despair, fate avenged Sophia Dorothea. The Princess was also avenged on the horrible Platens. The Count, blind for six years, was dying wretchedly. The Countess, stricken by a hideous disease, disfigured, abandoned, haunted by her crime, confessed it on her deathbed to a pastor. He in turn related the confession in a funeral oration which, according to Palmblad, was deposited in the Berlin archives.

There is almost nothing left of the Hanover of the Elector Ernst August and the Electress Sophia. The Alte Schloss and the Leinenschloss have disappeared. Herrenhausen was three-quarters destroyed by the bombs of the Electress' descendants. But by an eloquent turn of fate, Celle is intact. Leaving the highway for the road to Celle, one seems to have been put under a spell and transported to another country and another time. Here and there out of the twilight mists loom strange dwellings of a deep red-brown color. The town is unchanged and delightful, almost Dutch in style. It is Sophia Dorothea's town. The Princess walked through its small streets. The houses are painted from top to bottom with figures from folklore, and people used to lean out of their Gothic windows to watch the Princess pass. The park, with its century-old trees, is still there, and so is the chapel in which Sophia Dorothea's unfortunate marriage was celebrated. Her body lies in the vault now, but after how many vicissitudes! By order of George I she was to have been hastily buried at Ahlden with no ceremony of any kind. But the gravediggers dug in vain; the spongy ground filled with water. The coffin had to be brought back into the castle, where it was left under a few handfuls of sand until the day when the superstitious Duchess of Kendal, Mélusine von Schulenburg, was alarmed to see a crow fly over her head. She took the crow for the soul of Sophia Dorothea and demanded that she be given a decent burial. Thanks to Mélusine, the Duchess of Ahlden lies close to her parents in the duchy which never ceased to miss her. At Ahlden she visited the poor, was loved by everyone, built a church, and did good works. She was beloved by her little town. Count Schulenburg-Osterrode, the anonymous author of a romantic biography entitled *Die Herzogin von Ahlden*, managed shortly before 1800 to question an old woman of the region who remembered having seen the Princess pass, looking very beautiful, dressed in black, and wearing many diamonds.

The passing centuries have avenged Sophia Dorothea. If she could have looked at the beginning of the present century from beyond the grave, the repudiated, disgraced, and imprisoned Princess would have smiled to see the two great thrones of Europe occupied by her great-grandchildren: Queen Victoria and Kaiser Wilhelm II.

George Louis of Hanover King of England (George I)

George the First knew nothing and desired to know
nothing; did nothing and desired to do nothing; and
the only good thing that is told of him is that he
wished to restore the Crown to his hereditary
successor.

Doctor Johnson

As Queen Anne's strength declined, confusion overtook
the kingdom. Since the death of her son, the Queen's
mind was becoming clouded and she resorted increasingly to brandy.[1] The favorites fought bitterly at court.
Lady Abigail Masham, whom the Duchess of Marlborough had unwisely introduced to the Queen at the
little country palace of Kensington, finally evicted her
protectress, and this, in 1711, brought about the disgrace
of the Duke himself. Well-loved and all-powerful,
this Abigail kept a tight hold on the royal privy purse,
so much so that the Queen spent nothing for herself and
refused to buy the diamond (later known as the Regent
diamond) that Pitt had brought back from Madras.

---

[1] Herbert Paul, *Queen Anne*, 1906.

Never before had there been so much drinking, cheating, laughing, swearing, hunting, gambling, sword play, hanging, or robbing, under the trees of Hyde Park. Never before had there been so much brilliant writing, such coarse insults, or so much risk of being consigned to the Tower of London and of having one's property confiscated. Bigoted and illiterate, Anne found herself presiding over the most brilliant period for literature since Shakespeare's time, for among her subjects were Addison, Swift, Pope, Locke, Newton, Gay, Congreve, Defoe, Lord Chesterfield, Wycherley, Vanbrugh.

While the Pretender's remaining supporters were still negotiating if not for their future at least for their flight through the intermediary of Father Gaultier, a Frenchman, the shrewder among them crossed the North Sea and hurried to Hanover. "Hanover has become a little England," wrote the Duchess of Orleans. Toland, who went there on an official mission, described this mad race toward the power to be.[2] Lord Clarendon had no sooner arrived in Hanover than three messengers followed in haste. They brought the news that Queen Anne had just died after an unduly heated discussion with the Earl of Oxford. She was stricken with apoplexy like the Electress two months before her. According to Malortie, the English ambassador heard the news from one of the messengers as he was returning from dinner at Fantaisie, the residence of the Kilmanseggs. The ambassador is said to have immediately gone to Herrenhausen to awaken the Elector so as to be the first to salute him with his new title of King of England.

The taciturn George Louis lowered his head as if he had just heard some very bad news.

---

[2] Toland, *Account of the Courts of Prussia and Hanover.*

During August of 1714, envoys from all the courts of Europe came to Hanover to congratulate the king. The most zealous of his subjects were Lord Halifax, Albemarle, Marlborough, Lord Clarendon, and Lord Dorset. Men of letters such as Addison or John Gay also came to Hanover, ever ready to draft a pamphlet. "Write about the new king, it can't do any harm," was Pope's advice to Gay.[3]

The month of August was spent in preparations for departure. Finally, preceded by his suite, George I reluctantly set out.

The great-grandson through the female line of the Stuart King James I had no desire to leave Germany and take possession of his new kingdom. If he was not loved there, he hardly loved it either. Having won the grand prize, he indifferently put the winning ticket in his pocket and thought no more about it. Who, apart from Mlle. Schulenburg, could have warmed this unattractive icicle? In London people sang:

Over, over, Hanover, over!

Put in your claim before it's too late!

Or: "May King George protect us from Pope and Pretender!" It was the only prayer uttered in most of the kingdom. The God of the High Anglican Church, and of the quietists, Arians, Presbyterians, Methodists, Anabaptists, and Quakers had answered their prayers by granting them a Protestant king from among so many Catholic candidates. "It is the greatest miracle of our History," a Whig said. George I's religion enabled the English to overlook his faults and the fact that for them he was the petty prince of an almost unknown land.

This sovereign never appreciated the honor that was done him to reign over a victorious England, a country

---

[3] P. F. Gaye, *John Gay* (1938).

rich enough to have paid all the expenses of the Grand Coalition, having ruined Louis XIV, bled France, and imposed a lasting peace on her terms at Utrecht.

At the beginning of September 1714, high tides had brought bad weather. But a fortnight later it began to improve, announced at first by the slower movement of clouds from the west, patches of sun around midday, and a sky which grew more blue by the hour, as did people's disappointment at the shortness of the summer. The surface of the Thames was suddenly less muddy and became tinged with silver; the pigeons of Cheapside and the Stock Market dared to mingle their cooing with the endless laughing of the gulls.

The Thames ceased to be a sewer the color of stout, and once again became a royal way. It became dotted with barges flying streamers and full of musicians, and with the red and green forty-oared waterbuses lying alongside the latticed gates through which the palaces of the Strand had access to the river. Like a freshly laid ostrich egg, the limestone dome of the brand new St. Paul's Cathedral rose over a blackened City of London and a white Westminster. In the old City of Dick Whittington and the guilds, with its medieval red-brick and half-timbered houses behind the Roman wall, the Gothic gables and the towers of the guildhall were disappearing one by one before the spate of recent Neoclassical pediments, Baroque façades, and white steeples built a few decades earlier, after the Great Fire, by the young architects of the end of the previous century.

The Great Fire of 1666 was forgotten. Fifty years had snuffed out the memory of it. The Great Plague was also forgotten. Cripplegate, Aldgate, and Bishopsgate, huddled behind the Cathedral, were now eclipsed by the handsome new quarters of Soho, Leicester, and St. James, which led up to the old abbey at Westminster, beyond the Admiralty and on to Whitehall, toward the fields of Chelsea and the meadows of Kensington.

Beyond London's only bridge, an old one on which there were houses and shops, close to the Tower with its watery moats and dry ditches that were used as menageries for wild animals, in front of this white Tower dear to all Londoners, the yeomen of the guard, the Beefeaters, stood watch, their halberds on their shoulders, at the wicket gates leading to the sinsiter fortress built by William the Conqueror.

Suddenly, a twenty-one-cannon salute, somewhat muffled by the damp weather, sounded toward the east, in the direction of Greenwich.

"This time it must really be him!" cried the forty oarsmen of the Lord Mayor's ceremonial barge. They had been waiting at their benches since the previous evening for the new sovereign to arrive. After a difficult, four-day crossing, he entered a London that was ready to receive him. Already waiting around the royal coach were the Lords in their ermine robes and scarlet caps, the members of the House of Commons, the sheriffs and aldermen, the high-ranking clergymen in their robes of office, the pursuivants and heralds, the thirty-four Knights of the Bath, the mace-bearers bearing their silver gilt maces on their shoulders, the kettle-drummers flanked by the grenadiers of the Guard. Drawn by eight horses whose harness gleamed with gilded enrichments, the coach was to take the King from his boat to the ancient and gloomy palace of St. James, where he would reside.

After the salvos had died away, and when the bells of St. Mary Le Bow had stopped pealing, the first measures of a composition by Handel echoed across a river now swarming with thousands of small boats. There were boats that brought travelers from ocean-going ships to the city, there were escort ships, boats that continuously ferried people from bank to bank of the river, and finally boats packed with curious onlookers. Spectators also lined the steep riverbank, the quaysides, the steps, the dry docks. They even clustered under the pilings of the jetties and piers.

All Gin Lane was there—those who drank straight from the bottle, and those who drank from the cask. People full of gin mingled with harlots on holiday and with the tramps who slept the night under the arches of Covent Garden, Quakers who "thee'd" and "thou'd" everyone, bearded rabbis, Huguenot refugees, hack writers, bagpipers, shoeshine boys, West Indian sailors, and even blacker chimney sweeps, out-of-work actors, incurables from the hospitals of Southwark, and poor people clad in the blue uniform of the almshouse of Westminster. The cries of the hawkers were everywhere: "Buy my eels!" shouted the sellers of jellied eels, offering their wattle trays. Others drowned them out crying, "Oysters, oysters!" or "Hot puddings!"

Outspoken comments passed from boat to boat. The common people, whose only distraction was the hangings at Tyburn, reveled in the novel spectacle of an accession to the throne.

"Queen Anne is dead, and her nephew George I is arriving at last."

"He took a hell of a long time coming from Germany!"

"He's coming along backwards."

"As though he missed Hanover."

"Seems he's not very handsome, our new sovereign."

"And foul-tempered to boot," said a boatman at the Old Bridge.

"At home they call him 'pig head.' "

"A German pig head, that's twice as bad!"

Like the Roman slaves who had the right to insult conquering heroes on their way to the Capitol, to remind them to stay humble, the boatmen on the Thames for a century had had the privilege of abusing their sovereigns without risking the pillory.

"All I ask of this George is not to be a damned Papist like his uncles!"

"It's pretty bad his bringing up those German rats, but it's a lot better than monks from Rome!"

September 19, 1714

Morning chocolate was being served at the house of the poet Alexander Pope.

In the shade of an ancient cedar at Chiswick, a country district close to London, half a dozen bewigged gentlemen drank their morning chocolate. The day was emphatically beautiful, like a Dryden poem, and the last roses still had their summer colors. A young hunchback, who had an engaging air about him despite a forehead frequently furrowed by headaches, closed the manuscript of a translation of *The Iliad*, which he had just read aloud in his fine voice. His translation would definitely confirm the celebrity he had acquired three years ago with his *Essay on Cricism*.

The aged Wycherley said: "It is at dawn, the rosy-fingered, that one must savor the divine Homer. Was he not describing for us the dawn of the world?"

Alexander Pope tightened the cord around his black-

and-red-striped satin dressing gown, took off his white cotton nightcap, and bowed to thank his listeners.

"I am most happy to have pleased you," he said. "My only regret is that so many of our friends are absent as a result of the troubled times in which we live. Those who governed England yesterday are today in the Tower, or conspiring in France. . . ."

"And our dear old Dean Swift, who was a Whig too soon and a Tory at the wrong time, is now back home in Ireland to breathe purer air after his dangerous involvement with Bolingbroke and Harvey. I fear we won't see him again in this decade."[4]

"Meanwhile our other faithful friend, Daniel Defoe, having had too much of prison and the pillory under Queen Anne, has preferred to slip away on a secret mission. In the service of one half the police and sought by the other half, his life was more turbulent than his *Reasons for Being Against the House of Hanover*. His existence rather resembles the disputes of our valets and chambermaids who do not argue about the pudding or the beef, but about the rights of George I or the Pretender.

"Poor Defoe managed to be hated by both sides, . . ." said Steele.

Congreve added, "I will miss Defoe with his hooked nose, his jutting chin, and his devilish wit."

Richard Steele inquired about John Gay.

    Ever Gay
    In fair weather
    or foul,

hummed Pope. "Our Gay prefers fine weather and has

---

[4] Had Swift been at this meeting, he would certainly have related it in his *Journal to Stella* better than I have done here.

gone with Lord Clarendon to Hanover to warm himself in the rising sun—King George I. Addison has done the same."

"And yet we have learned what it costs to dabble in the affairs of state," grumbled Vanbrugh. "Politics is a plague for authors."

Pope burst out laughing.

"Especially when the throne is shaky, and ministers cover themselves in both camps, and only madmen remain where they are in the asylum at Bedlam . . . because they are chained there!"

A maid brought frothy ale in a black leather jug and took away the empty chocolate pot.

"We are living in the continental manner," Congreve concluded. "England had the choice between a Papist king living at French expense, or another, a Lutheran, living in Hanover. England took the German because he is Protestant. Religion is our real country."

"Although I am above all an Arcadian shepherd, I am a Catholic," said the host. "My name Pope means what it says. However, I declare that after having beheaded a king, tried a republic, wavered between two queens and three pretenders, England can no longer deprive her people of George I, whom they are demanding."

"The more so since George I is getting on. It is reassuring to think that he has passed fifty, an age at which a king no longer has any teeth."

"Defoe has said: 'Titles are shadows and crowns are empty things.' Consider our monarchs in succession: Charles II without issue; James II, a Catholic; his first daughter, Mary, had no children; Anne, his second daughter, lost hers. Catholicism, sterility, and death have created a vacuum around the throne of England. So we have deserved George I."

"He is a brute and an icicle, by all accounts."

"Terribly unattractive," said Pulteney, filling his long clay pipe. "Queen Anne detested him and didn't want him for a husband when he came to London thirty-four years ago."

"All the same," said Pope, "among the hundreds of pretenders of Stuart blood, she finally chose him as heir."

"What do we know about him?" asked Congreve.

"What do the Amsterdam newspapers say? They are always so well informed."

"What does it matter! Hanover is of no more interest to the English public than China."

"Is he married?" asked Arbuthnot.

"I don't know. At all events, he is coming to us without a queen."

"Doubtless she has been dead for a long time," said Pope. "No one ever talks about her."

"Perhaps she was only a morganatic wife and he is ashamed of her?"

"Or perhaps mad, and he has hidden her?"

"In any case, there was a wife because he has a daughter who will be Queen of Prussia and a son who is our Prince of Wales."

"Well then, what happened to their mother?"

"You can ask His Majesty, my dear Pope, when you ask for a royal subscription to the first volume of your *Iliad*!"

"Protocol wisely forbids asking questions of sovereigns, and in any case ours would not answer," Pope replied.

"Is he dumb?"

"No," said Pope, while pulling up the three pairs of socks which were slipping down his thin calves. "George I of England does not know a single word of English."

"How will he manage to speak to his ministers?"

"He won't speak to them."

"What an excellent definition of parliamentary rule!" Congreve exclaimed.

"All the same, when he receives his Prime Minister, surely they won't communicate like deaf-mutes? How will they talk to each other?"

"In Latin."

At this time the order of succession to the throne was to throw whole nations into disorder. Our own affairs of state today with their reversals of alliances, their scientific discoveries, or their assassinations, still have a certain quality of the unexpected. But we are deprived of the melodramatic spectacle of nations suddenly enriched by unexpected inheritances, or sacked by the wording of a will.

The continental invasion of England, dreamed of since 1066 by so many conquerors, was to be accomplished, for the first time, by Germans at the beginning of the eighteenth century. Moreover, it would be a legitimate, more or less peaceful invasion by virtue of a perfectly proper inheritance. A foreign dynasty was on the point of establishing itself, and was not only accepted but requested by the majority of British opinion in an age in which religious faith weighed more heavily than national passions. Henry VIII still cast a shadow on the palace of St. James. By simple accidents of birth and natural deaths, this remote dynasty would be sent to take over with full title to the succession. The house of Hanover which would annex England, would need nearly a century to accustom itself to this fabulous inheritance and nearly a century and a half before it lost to Prussia and to the grasping Bismark the corner of Germany from which its kings came.

Was this slow start a clever stroke springing from George I's desire to test English public opinion before landing, or was he really unable to tear himself away from Hanover? The daughter of the "wicked countess Platen," who was to take over her mother's title, was quite ready to accompany George I, but her creditors prevented her from entering Holland. However, she managed to join the traveling party and rejoin the King at The Hague. Mlle. Schulenburg tried to pull George I back by the coattails. She did not wish to leave Germany for a barbaric country where she maintained that it was customary to behead kings. In vain George pointed out to her that the so-called regicides were indeed his supporters. She clung to Hanover, declaring that at fifty-five one does not change countries. Her lover had to promise her an abundance of gold and jewels. What finally decided her was her unwillingness to leave Madame Kilmansegg alone with the King. But the King had to assure her that there would be no trouble and that they would live in England as in a conquered country.

George was almost right: the Jacobites, overtaken by the rapidity of events, had done nothing; Louis XIV had reached the age of seventy-eight and was no longer a threat, and the Whigs, who had been biding their time for four years, would offer a triumphal welcome in the name of parliamentary principles to a virtually absolute monarch.

On September 16 George I embarked at Oranie Polder, Holland, aboard the *Peregrine*. His ship was accompanied by an honor squadron which was soon joined by the bulk of the British fleet. He arrived in Greenwich on the 18th. After having bestowed on his son the title of Prince of Wales on the 20th, he entered London.[5]   On the 21st he held his first formal reception in St. James' palace; on the 22nd he convened the Privy Council to form a new cabinet.   On October 18th, he was crowned in Westminster.

The crowds that watched him go by in his coach found him heavy and graceless.   Like Horace Walpole they would have said: "By no means an inviting object."   In fact he looked much the same as he did when the Princess Palatine wrote of him from Versailles on April 22, 1702: "A surly and two-faced egotist . . . lacking any natural goodness, making no attempt to appear handsome, interested in no one . . . a dry, disagreeable, avaricious, and haughty man."

The roads were so dreadful that planks had to be laid down on them so that people could reach the houses, and coaches would often fall through into the basements. But nothing stopped travelers: mohawks (the skinheads of the time) would attack them, but that did not prevent the gay parties.   You just had to bring along your dog and your saber.   The distressing sadness of London after the Plague and the Puritanism of Cromwell's time were ended.   A beginning was made on paving and lighting the streets; elegant dwellings were being built at Piquidilla.[6]   Among the attractions of George I's London were the purlieus and the bordellos with their bawds known as "mothers," the shady bagnios, the ridottos, the alfrescos, the coteries where group sex was practiced and a mixture of beer and champagne was drunk. There was boxing, golf, cricket, games of bowls on the

---

[5] For a detailed description of the entry into London, see *Mémoires du règne de Georges 1ᵉʳ*, The Hague, 1729.
[6] Th. Burke, *The Streets of London*, 1940.

bowling greens, cock and dog fights which drew the young bloods, disreputable lords, drunks, West Indian pages and beggars. One custom was to throw things at cockerels confined in an enclosure until they were dead, or to shut them up in an earthenware pot at the top of a mast and shoot at them. Macaulay says that there were grouse shoots along Regent Street. There were hunting clubs in the center of the city: ducks would be released on a pond, and anyone with a few pence would be allowed to release his dogs on them. The rich "joyfully insulted poverty" (Fielding). Artisans worked fifteen hours a day, and their daughters had to so-licit at street corners at the risk of being publicly whipped. For the least infringement people would be clapped in irons, or have a hand burned, or be deported to Amer-ica.[7]

In the first of his lectures devoted to the four Georges,[8] Thackeray described the arrival of George I in England with admirable verve:

He brought with him a compact body of Germans whose society he loved, his faithful German chamberlains, his German secretaries; his negroes captive of his bow and spear in Turkish wars; his two ugly elderly German favorites, Mesdames of Kielmansegge and Schulen-berg. I am a citizen waiting at Greenwich pier, say, and cry hurrah for King George, and yet I can scarcely keep my countenance and help laughing at the enormous absurdity of this advent!

Here we are, all on our knees. Here is the Archbishop of Canterbury prostrating himself to the head of his

---

[7] J. Dennis, *The Age of Pope*. London, 1909.
[8] W. M. Thackeray, *The Four Georges*.

*Church, with Kielmansegge and Schulenberg with their
ruddled cheeks grinning behind the defenser of the faith.
Here is my Lord Duke of Marlborough kneeling too, the
greatest warrior of all times; he who betrayed King
William—betrayed James II—betrayed Queen Anne—
betrayed England to the French, the Elector to the Pretender, the Pretender to the Elector; and here are my
Lords Oxford and Bolingbroke. The Great Whig Gentlemen made their bows and congees with proper docorum
and ceremony, but yonder keen old Schemer knows
the value of thin loyalty. "Loyalty" he must think—it
is absurd! There are fifty nearer heirs to the throne than
I am. I am but an accident, and you fine Whig gentlemen take me for your own sake, not for mine. You Tories
hate me; you archbishop, smirking on your knees, and
prating about Heaven, you know I don't care a fig for
your Thirty-nine Articles . . . you, my Lords Bolingbroke and Oxford—you know you were conspiring
against me a month ago. Come, my good Melusina, come,
my honest Sophia! let us have some oysters and some
Rhine wine, and some pipes afterwards: let us make the
best of our situation; let us take what we can get[9] and
leave these brawling, brawling lying English to shout,
and fight, and cheat in their own way!*

George I was hated and scorned by his British subjects,
although the Hanoverians respected and loved him.
Did he deserve this ill feeling? He was a brave soldier,
a good general, and an excellent administrator. Can he
be reproached for the way he governed England? He
never governed it. He had the wisdom to let it govern
itself, which it did very well under the leadership of

---

[9] He might have said of London, as Blücher did in 1814: "What a city to pillage!"

the remarkable Robert Walpole. Walpole detested war in all forms, civil, foreign, and colonial, and he had the good sense always to avoid it. Moreover war was no longer necessary. The rebellion had been put down; France, the hereditary enemy, had been crushed and, better still, had joined the English alliance. It was a time when one could relax. England's awful pauperism, the atrocious exploitation of the working class, would come later when the great landowners realized that it was easier to raise cattle than to grow wheat. At that point they turned their wheat fields into pasturage, starving the rural population and driving the country folk to the factories that opened everywhere with the discovery of the uses of coal. From that moment on England was industrialized. But under George I it was still an agricultural country and its people were contented. Reading contemporary correspondence and the gazettes is enough to give one an idea of that contentment.

George I presided over the Council only once, for he understood nothing about English internal affairs. Prudence and sluggishness were his master cards. He allowed his ministers to govern and concerned himself with foreign policy, for he knew Europe well, while the English had little interest in it. He contented himself with settling the frequent conflicts that arose between the Whig ministers and his German ministers. This narrowminded sovereign quickly understood that in England he could no longer be the absolute monarch he was on the Continent. What a change St. James Palace was for him after Hanover, where the castle fixed the time of day and where the city's clocks were respectfully set by the Elector's watch. Like one of his ancestors, George I could have said: "The only great man in my duchy is the man to whom I am speaking, and then only for as long as I continue speaking to him."

In addition to foreign affairs, George also devoted himself to military affairs. He was shocked by the state of the English army, which had been used mainly for riot control. There was no permanent army, for according to English tradition, it would have been considered a threat to civil liberties. Queen Anne had left him a force of only 8,000 men, which was scarcely half the size of the Hanoverian army. Moreover, it was a heterogeneous and undisciplined group, and soldiers fought each other in the streets. There were three barracks for the whole of England, and three regiments were stationed in Flanders[10] for all continental wars. George's new subjects lacked the military spirit; there were no fanfares, no reveilles to the sound of fifes as there had been in Hanover, where each time the princes sallied forth trumpets and cymbals announced the event, and where the Elector even went to the toilet to the sound of an orchestra. The soldier-king felt very far away from his fine regiments which would parade in squads three deep and thirty-two across.

The king reorganized the army, setting up fighting units, and separating the civil from the military authorities, for since the time of Cromwell they had frequently overlapped. He gave the infantry flintlocks, created an army headquarters, had the men perform swift, German-style maneuvers, including attacking columns, perfect discipline, and firing at will. He purged the officers' corps, "the worst in Europe," according to Chesterfield, and forbade the train of coaches that encumbered the line of march. In a word, George I allowed his kingdom to benefit from the genius of Gustavus Adolphus, the true father of modern warfare before Frederick II. Thanks to the King, England profited by the whole

---

[10] *The Oxford History of England*, Vol. II (1939).

of German military experience from the Thirty Years' War to the recent battles with the Turks. These excellent measures would bear fruit during the Napoleonic wars.

George I gave occasional galas or assemblies, but he did not willing grant audiences. He had "smoke-filled room" sessions for himself alone, with one of his two Mamelukes behind him stuffing his Dutch pipe, and the other holding the delft spittoon. He lived in isolation with his women. He had become very ugly, his large nose imprisoned between two deep wrinkles that resembled parentheses, his cheeks falling almost to his chin. He was seen in public only at the theater in the Haymarket to which he would go in his sedan chair carried by his two Turks. He never missed an opera by Händel, his former *Kapellmeister* in Hanover, whom he rediscovered with pleasure despite the fact that Händel had left Hanover, where he was badly paid. Fourteen years later the composer became a naturalized Englishman. In 1717, for his birthday, the King commissioned Händel to write the "Water Music." Signor Händel had just had an immense success with his opera *Rinaldo*. The air *"Cara sposa"* from the first act was being played on every harpsichord. Now Händel became reconciled with Hanover and the new King confirmed the pension of 200 pounds that Queen Anne had granted him. George could not do without the composer and took him along when he went to Hanover the following year.

Life was organized in the German manner, with a German timetable, German servants, German concubines ("the seraglio of hideous German prostitutes," as the Jacobites put it), German ministers, Counts Bernstorff and Robethon, a former Huguenot refugee, Count Platen, von Kilmansegg, the Master of the Horse, Baron von Goritz (the only honest man in the lot, according to Lady Mary Wortley Montagu), Baron von Bothmer, Hanover's representative in London under Queen Anne. Just as William III had had his Dutch favorites, George I had his German favorites, although they were less handsome.

Mlle. Schulenburg, who was getting to look more and more like a Goya portrait, was either the mistress or the morganatic wife of the King; no one knew which. With her was her daughter, the Countess Kilmansegg, who already looked like a fading Rubens, and who was either the King's daughter or Königsmark's; no one was sure. It was even whispered that she was also the King's mistress. She was as fat as Schulenburg was thin, she had to be laced into her corsets as a chicken is trussed, and she dressed badly and gaudily. Her face was bright with crimson rouge and her eyes were blackened under heavy eyebrows the color of coal. Kilmansegg was nicknamed the "elephant" or "Elephant and Castle," and her mother the "maypole." When they passed, the crowd would shout: "Down with the German rates." Thereupon Mlle. Schulenburg would lean out of her carriage and cry in bad English: "Good people, we are here for your good. . . ." "For our goods!" the crowd would shout back. Schulenburg lacked the presence of mind of Louise de Keroualle, the French-born Duchess of Portsmouth who was Charles II's mistress and who was also detested by the populace. When the crowd would shout at her, she would reply: "Me no whore, me no whore."

The King would contemplate the demonstrators with his usual sullenness and frown from the depths of the carriage. "The English air made him even harder," wrote the Princess Palatine.

Already public opinion was accusing the seraglio of laying hands on Queen Anne's jewels. The whole royal entourage meddled and sold themselves to the highest bidder. Even the two Muslems, Mahomet and Mustapha, peddled their influence.

Horace Walpole, who at the age of eight was received by the King, stated that he did not remember the features of the Duchess of Kendal (Mlle. Schulenburg), who was present during the audience. Of the Countess of Darlington (Countess Kilmansegg) he remembered: "Two flashing black eyes under high arching black brows; an ocean of neck which so spread that it merged with the rest of her body; her corset withheld nothing tempting." On May 27, 1721, *Mist's Journal* carried the statement: "We are being ruined by loose women, and what is worse by hideous loose women." This earned the author a fine and a prison sentence.

1714

Twenty years later. . . . Sophia Dorothea was still imprisoned at Ahlden. In England, where it is unbecoming to ask questions, no one spoke of her. People remained silent through indifference, or lack of curiosity, or through good breeding. They still believed that the King was a widower, and contemporary historians did not even mention the name of the Duchess of Ahlden. Nothing would be published about her in England before 1773, and what was published then followed Pollnitz (whose *Histoire secrette* was written in 1732). That romantic biography interested only romantics. The *Mémoires de Sophie Dorothée* (1845) spoke of a supposed *Journal* written by a so-called secretary, translated from German, and published in 1821. There was also talk of manuscripts lost in Berlin, and of others forgotten in Brunswick, or hidden at Celle or Hanover. The *Mémoires* mentioned a *Précis de mon destin et de ma prison*, supposedly by Sophia Dorothea. They say that the manuscript of this work was given by the author before her death "to persons worthy of trust." The introduction to this *Précis*, and of a diary included with it, is alleged to have contained details about the Duchess of Celle and the origins of the d'Olbreuse family that only Sophia Dorothea could have known.[11] *The Present State of Britain* (1716) by Chamberlayne describes the history of the house of Hanover in detail, but does not even mention Sophia Dorothea's name. In 1726, Kerr of Kersland, the British consul in Amsterdam, published a *Voyage aux Cours de Celle et de Hanovre* (*Journey to the Courts of Celle and Hanover*) in which he refered to a "beautiful princess, the sole heir to Celle," which was enough to cause him serious trouble.[12]

Doran, in his *Lives of the Queens of England*, wrote that before leaving Hanover George I tried to effect a reconciliation with his wife. There is nothing to prove this, and the King's whole character suggests the contrary. The break was final, and with the death of the Duchess of Celle, the solitude of the confined Princess was total. The few links that Sophia Dorothea still had with her daughter, the Queen of Prussia, were ended, because the Duchess of Celle had served as the intermediary. When in 1725 the Queen of Prussia came to Hanover to visit her father, George I, during the course of one of his trips to the Continent, she was forbidden by her husband, King Frederick, to visit Ahlden.

---

[11] *Mémoires de Sophia Dorothée* (Preface, pp. 10 and 11), 1845.
[12] *Ibid.*

The only thing George I did not deny the prisoner of Ahlden was doctors. The *Mémoires de Sophie Dorothée* relate that he had always had doubts about the legality of his divorce and that he feared that his lawsuit would be reconsidered and that Sophia Dorothea would rejoin him and have herself crowned queen. This was to misjudge the character of the Princess, and his fear was groundless. But the King was haunted by another fear, an incurable and chronic one that gave this brave but superstitious soldier goose flesh. Horace Walpole explained the cause: Many years before a French clairvoyant named Deborah had been received at the court of Hanover and had predicted to George Louis that he would follow his wife to the grave within twelve months of her death. It is no wonder that George I took as much care of Sophia Dorothea's health as of his own.[13] Doctors followed one another to Ahlden and sent written reports of their consultations to the Palace of St. James. Was it not a troubled conscience that made the King of England sweat with fear at night?

---

[13] While allowing that Horace Walpole's information might be tenuous, it must be remembered that this account came from his father, Sir Robert Walpole, Prime Minister of King George I.

11 / The Stuart Rebellion

The unfortunate Stuarts, parading their misfortunes higher than their white cockades, had bad luck of the sort that occurs in novels. They were children spoiled by fickleness, tactlessness, financial problems, and the most antiquated type of ceremonial life. Their comic misfortunes, their notorious and foolish tardiness, and their abortive conspiracies are more revealing than triumphs. The blessed Stuarts were endowed with all the glamour that the Hanoverians lacked. They had indomitable pride; they behaved badly with grandeur; they faced the worst disgraces with elegance; they were as generous as beggars; their unyielding sense of nobility set them off against the English aristocracy, whose authenticity was so doubtful. "The great English lords are of a blood as mixed as our dukes here. There are scarcely two of them who can prove four quarters in their coat of arms." (Princess Palatine, letter from Versailles, March 17, 1697.) The Stuarts were sort of like the Poles of the Western World, always regretted in England as soon as they fell, bewailed by this ponderous Anglo-Saxon people who envied their light touch. (For the Stuarts, at least, unheated winters in Saint-Germain and pensions from Louis XIV were still less humiliating than handing around the hat at the International Monetary Fund.) In a cynical and un-Stuart vein, the Princess Palatine wrote on September

13, 1690: "The good King James II should have had a little religion like me rather than lose three kingdoms as a result of his bigotry." Charles de Brosses equaled the style of Saint-Simon when he wrote about the Stuarts, with the grandness of an inscription on a tombstone: "So many people secretly back this faction less because they support it than because they would be upset if the house of Stuart were to die out so that they would not be able to point it out from afar to the reigning King."[1]

There were 16 million Frenchmen and only 5 to 6 million Englishmen when George I acceded to the throne. But France had been bled white and was bankrupt, while England, although temporarily deep in debt, had her manpower intact. Any statesman could have been proud of these two most intelligent statements made by Robert Walpole. The first, a cynical one, he made while observing a group of members of Parliament: "Each of these consciences has its price." The second, which should serve as a motto to the French, was made at the end of the Grand Alliance: "Forty thousand men killed in Europe, and not one Englishman."

Blood had flowed in the United Kindgom only during the civil war known as the Rebellion of 1715, while a long period of calm began for Europe thanks to the Franco-British entente, which had received the blessings of the Free Masons and the Regent. The Treaty of Utrecht had just put an end to the hospitality that Louis XIV had offered to the Stuarts when they had been expelled from England. After Utrecht, James II had to leave France and seek refuge in Lorraine. Surrounded

---

[1] It is also worth reading Voltaire's fine pages about the Stuarts in the *Siècle de Louis XIV*, Chap. 15.

by English spies, it became difficult for him to cross the Channel quickly. The Jacobite party in England was divided, as were the Tories, while the united Whigs had just come into power, and for a long time, thanks to their triumphant victory at a general election. Out of hatred for George I the Tories declared: "If you do not want to see the Pretender become King of England, make him the Elector of Hanover first." But their ill humor went no further than this outburst. Bolingbroke and the Earl of Oxford were prosecuted for the part they and the Duke of Ormond played in the Treaty of Utrecht. Bolingbroke had slipped away to France, and Ormond advised Oxford to follow his example. The Earl refused:

"Farewell, Oxford . . . soon to be without a head," said Ormond.

"Farewell, Duke . . . already without a duchy," Oxford replied.

Late as always, the Pretender (whom prudent men called the Knight of St. George so as not to compromise themselves) procrastinated once again. At the crucial moment he had to postpone his departure because he had caught the measles. (Nothing is more tragic than a ridiculous accident.) A price of £100,000 was put on his head.

The chosen ground was Scotland, a non-Anglican country more attached to its earlier kings. John Erskine, second Earl of Mar, was a Scotsman initially faithful to George I. He had hurried to Greenwich to greet him, but the King had turned his back on him, and the Earl returned to Scotland. One day, at the end of a hunt, he proposed to the other hunters that now they should hunt the Hanoverian, not the fox. His proposal was greeted with cheers. Mar was made the Pretender's chief of staff and began to gather troops. At first there were few of them, but soon they outnumbered the Royalists, particularly when the north of England rebelled as well. Lord Derwentwater, a twenty-four-year-old Catholic, led the rebels in Northumberland. Scattered islands of revolt appeared in the west, particularly at Bath, Bristol, and Plymouth.

The Whigs reacted swiftly. The Duke of Argyle took command of the national armies. The Habeas Corpus act was suspended, and 6,000 men were recalled from Holland. Soon part of the Jacobite army was surrounded at Preston, while the other half was defeated at Dumblain and at the battle of Sheriffmuir. The strategy at the latter action is still famous because the right wings of both armies were victorious at the same time, which caused Argyle to remark that his right hand knew not what his left hand was doing. The Highlanders were formidable warriors, but their clan rivalries prevented them from making a victory of a favorable battle.

On December 6, 1715, the "King over the water," as the English called the Pretender, came over from France, landing in Peterhead. He was disguised as a French naval officer and brought with him a handful of supporters. The Regent had not wished to support him openly, for he was anxious not to fall out with England.

The Pretender was not loved. His supporters found him broody, peevish, and indecisive. He ordered a retreat and returned to France after a rebellion that had lasted five months.

Repression was severe, but there were no excesses, although the Jacobites alleged that the Whigs had spattered the royal ermine with blood. There were a large number of arrests: seven peers were condemned to death and their estates confiscated, but only two were executed, of which one was Derwentwater. Three were pardoned and two escaped from the Tower of London, one of them clad in his wife's clothes after she had visited him. Twenty-two soldiers were hung in Lancashire, and four in London, but the majority of them were deported to America. When Lord Nithdale's escape was announced to George I, he said calmly: "Good for him. Above all don't try to catch him."

Thackeray in *The Four Georges* argued that Scotland and the armies of the Pretender almost won. His novelist's imagination getting the better of him, this is how he portrayed such a victory and its consequences:

As one thinks of what might have been, how amusing the speculation is! We know how the doomed Scottish gentlemen came out at Lord Mar's summons, mounted the white cockade, that has been the flower of sad poetry ever since, and rallied round the ill-omened Stuart standard at Braemar. Mar, with 8,000 men, but 1,500 opposed to him, might have driven the enemy over to the Tweed, and taken possession of the whole of Scotland; but that the Pretender's Duke did not venture to move when the day was his own. Edinburgh Castle might have been in King James' hands; but that the men who were to escalade it stayed to drink his health at the tavern, and arrived two hours too late at the rendezvous under the castle walls. There was sympathy enough in the town—the projected attack seems to have been known there—Lord Mahon quotes Sinclair's account of a gentleman not concerned, that he was in a house that evening where eighteen of them were drinking as the facetious landlady said: "Powdering their hair" for the attack of the castle. Suppose they had not stopped to powder their hair? Edinburgh Castle and town and all Scotland were King James'. The north of England rises, and marches over Barnet Heath upon London. Wyndham is up in Somersetshire, Packington in Worcestershire, and Vivian in Cornwall. The Elector of Hanover and his hideous mistress, pack up the plate, and perhaps the crown jewels in London, and are off via Harwich and Helvoersluys, for dear old Deutschland. The King—God save him!—lands at Dover, with tumultuous applause; shouting multitudes, roaring cannon, the Duke of Marlborough weeping tears of joy, and all the bishops kneeling in the mud. . . . In a few years mass is said in St. Paul's; matins and vespers are sung in York Minster and Dr. Swift is turned out of his stalls and deanery house at St. Patrick's, to give place to Father Dominic, from Salamanca. All these changes were possible then, and once thirty years afterwards—all this we might have had, but for the pulveris exigui jactu, that little toss of powder for the hair which the Scotch conspirators stopped to take at the tavern. . . .

12 / Sophia Dorothea's son The Prince of Wales The Future George II of England

An English humorist once said: "George I could not have been such a bad man, for he never hated but three people: his mother, his wife, and his son."

A celebrated and mutual hatred existed between the King and George August, the Prince of Wales and the future George II. Unquestionably the King saw Sophia Dorothea in his son, for the child had her complexion, her shining eyes, her light brown hair, her handsome figure, her pride, her quick temper, and her gift for quick repartee. His father admitted as much when he once said: "He is impetuous but good-hearted." From his father the Prince of Wales got his taste of all things military, even though he was a peaceable sovereign. He was courageous and fought brilliantly at Oudenarde under Marlborough. As a young man he was aggressive to the point of nearly fighting a duel with his brother-in-law, the King of Prussia (whom he called "my brother-in-law the corporal"). He only refrained from running his brother-in-law through when it was pointed out to him how ridiculous it was for two future kings to be dueling at all.

George August was born in 1683 before Königsmark arrived in Hanover. Thus the nickname "little Königsmark," which he was given in certain Jacobite pamphlets, is pure calumny. All Europe spoke of the family feud. The Princess Palatine wrote: "I imagine that the King of England does not believe that the Prince of Wales is his, because if he did believe it he would not treat his only son so badly." Nevertheless, the suspicion that he was illegitimate weighed for a long time over the Prince of Wales. One day, during a reception in the Palace of St. James, the Prince of Wales was jostled by an illegitimate son of Charles II (George, ostensibly the son of the Duke of Newcastle). The Prince exclaimed loudly: "We walk over bastards here!" "My Lord," answered the offended party, "my father was as great a king as yours. As for our mothers, we had better not speak of them."

When George I first returned to Hanover, he was obliged against his will to name his son regent. Later he withdrew the title and named him only guardian of the kingdom of England. The father could never forgive the Prince for having succeeded in making himself popular with everyone. According to Horace Walpole, he even thought of sending his son off to America. John Morley, in his biography of Walpole, confirmed this when he wrote that on the death of the King a draft note on this matter had been found in his papers.

Here again we can recognize the influence of the dreadful Bernstorff, of whom Elisabeth-Charlotte d'Orléans wrote on June 9, 1718: "People in Paris are saying that

Bernstorff is the one who has set the King so violently against the Prince and Princess of Wales. He ought to be ashamed of himself to be German and to be more treacherous than an Englishmen. . . ."

When his second grandson, the Duke of Gloucester, was born, George I insisted on being a godfather, and chose the Duke of Newcastle as the second godfather. The Prince of Wales was furious and insulted the Duke by calling him a scoundrel. Thereupon George I ordered his son and daughter-in-law out of the palace and, with almost unbelievable callousness, refused the Prince the custody of his children, and even forbid the parents to see them. The Prince and his wife took up residence in Leicester House and, in the summer, at Richmond. There they became the center of the Tory opposition and of everything that was young, sparkling, and intelligent in London. Surrounded by a swarm of beautiful women, the famous "maids of honor," the Princess of Wales was the inspiration of the opposition throughout her life. The daughter of the Margrave of Brandenburg-Anspach, Caroline was married to the Prince of Wales in 1705, and lived to become a famous name in the history of England. She was learned, with a particular penchant for philosophy; she often used the crudest language, and to top it off she was the most beautiful woman of her time. She was feared by George I, who would curse "this she devil, the Princess!" When her husband became King she reigned alone and very well indeed during a two-year period when he was out of England, for he loved Hanover as much as his father did. Caroline's influence on her husband was unlimited. She even succeeded in imposing Robert Walpole on him despite the fact that George detested Walpole.

George I made no secret of his quarrel with his son.

The Princess Palatine wrote: "Paris asserts that George I intends to declare publicly that the Prince of Wales is not his son, and to spite him even more, he wants to marry Mlle. Schulenburg, who is at present the Duchess of Munster." The King certainly gave maximum publicity to his conflict with his son, officially informing all the courts of it, and depriving the Prince of his honor guard. The Prince wrote letter after letter in an attempt to get his children back. Robert Walpole tried to patch things up, but the Prince refused to return to his father's residence. In the end he visited the King, whose voice was heard through the doors saying: "*Votre conduite! Votre conduite!*" ("Your behavior! Your behavior!") (German royalty ruling England and conversing only in French; what a splendid time this was before the nationalism of the nineteenth century.) Lady Cowper wrote that father and son were seen together at a religious ceremony, but they were not speaking to one another. George I took advantage of the quarrel to tear up the will that Sophia Dorothea had made in favor of her children. Behind all these goings on one can imagine the evil influence of the King's "two ladies," whom the Prince hated as much as they hated him. Like the Princess Palatine, he must have thought that "courts are packs of rascals and strumpets."

George II's first act on the death of his father was to tear up his father's will under the nose of the Archbishop of Canterbury who, in accordance with protocol, had brought it to him so that it should be opened in his presence.

The shade of Sophia Dorothea hung over the hatred between father and son. There is no doubt that the Prince of Wales secretly loved his mother. As we have seen, he would have thrown himself into her arms at Ahlden if the commander of the castle, Baron von Bülow, had not forbidden him to enter. George II had all the papers relating to his father's divorce burned. Lady Suffolk told Horace Walpole that the prince secretly kept a portrait of his mother which he put on show once his father had died. He believed in Sophia Dorothea's innocence, but he never spoke of her. It is said that ghosts can pass though walls and mirrors; they pass much more easily through the arteries and the blood.[1]

---

[1] The anecdote showing George II putting his mother's portrait in its rightful place was also related by Lord Hervey in his *Mèmoirs*. According to him, the rumor in London was that George II would have called his mother to his side had she still been alive.

13 / The Ghost
of Sophia Dorothea
Is Avenged

George I was a constitutional king, but in the beginning his attitude was scarcely constitutional. He had only smiles for the Whigs while turning his back on the Tories. Bolingbroke was summarily banished; Parliament, which should have sat for six months longer under the terms of a recent law, was dissolved as soon as it had sworn allegiance to the King and had voted him personal and household expense money for the year. This did not prevent George I from presenting a bill for a large amount of back pay due that part of the Hanoverian army that had been engaged in the Grand Alliance. General elections swept the Whigs back in with an impressive majority.

Now the King had only to reign. He managed skillfully to maintain his position and make himself respected without being loved. George I had not sought the honor that had devolved upon him. In this delicate affair of the succession he had been very well advised of his mother's old friend Leibnitz, whose mind was not only scholarly but profoundly political, and of whom the King said: "He is a living dictionary." Unfortunately Leibnitz was not able to inspire George for long. He suffered from gout and, trying a remedy of his own making, he died within the hour.

The King's very indifference and ignorance helped him. Not knowing English, he soon ceased to preside over the Council, and allowed his ministers to govern.

Obtuse as he may have been, George I could not fail to understand that if Holland was a small England, Hanover for England was only a small Holland. The imperial military machine was most impressive when inactive, but its quarter of a million soldiers would only be seen in motion if England paid the bill for the war. George I did not turn up his nose at material wealth, and he must have seen that a heavy public debt did not prevent English boats from returning laden with riches from the Spanish colonies, thanks to smuggling and to loopholes in the Colonial Pact that encircled the Spanish Empire like a great wall of China. In France, Louis XIV ("the old machine," as Lord Stair had called him) was dead. The Regent and Dubois turned their country into the most accommodating neighbor imaginable. They drove the Pretender as far away as possible—from Bar-le-Duc to Avignon, and then to Italy. But this did not prevent George I "from hating France most wonderfully," to quote again from Lord Stair.

An English peace, similar to the one created by Wellington, reigned over the whole of Europe. The Triple Alliance signed at The Hague in 1717 united France, Holland, and England. One year later the Treaty of Madrid added Spain and it became the Quadruple Alliance. The North Sea was an English sea; Hanover had just bought Bremen and Verden (with English money, according to Chesterfield). In the Baltic, Sweden played a diminishing role as Russia looked increasingly westward.

In London one could still hear the occasional grumble: "No Hanover!" and in 1718 an attempt was made on the King's life. Despite these incidents, the English were beginning to become accustomed to this sovereign who tolerated the opposition and let the *Tatler* and the *Spectator* (20,000 copies) poke fun at him.

The image of the aging George I is inseparable from that of Lady Kendal. She had remained much as she was when she came off the boat—a thin German, impervious to England. The King shut himself up with her every afternoon from five to eight before going to the theater "with his ladies."[1] There he would leave the royal box empty and slip into another one, hiding behind Lady Kendal.[2] When they were together, the King would drink his mug of beer while she made paper cutouts— teapots, vases, flowers, all of paper. George would gaze at her in delight, seeing things only through the eyes of the Duchess, the "real queen of England." She had the nonchalant ways and calculated innocence of the great money grabbers. The only bits of paper she would not use for her découpage were the notes issued by the Bank of England, for her greed was boundless. According to Robert Walpole, "she would have sold the King's honor to the highest bidder for a shilling." Everyone who sought favors at court had to pass through her. When Bolingbroke tired of his exile in France and wanted to return home, he had to give Lady Kendal £11,000. When the post of Master of the Horse fell vacant upon the resignation of the Duke of Somerset, the Duchess drew

---

[1] Lady Cowper, *Diary*.
[2] H. Walpole.

the £7,500 salary that the post paid. A banker had to pay her £14,000 for the right to mint copper coins in Ireland. Gifts in kind poured in; the diplomatic corps ruined itself for her. Louis XV told Broglie, his envoy to London, to take special care of her because she had the King's ear.

She was said to be morganatically married to the King, and even to have been married by the Archbishop of York. She was steeped in good works and attended all services at the Lutheran church in London, flanked by the two nieces she had brought with her to England. One was the daughter of her brother; the other, Pétronille Mélusine von Schulenburg, was made Baroness Aldborough and Lady Walsingham, and later married the Earl of Chesterfield. This niece was probably the daughter of George I. Kendal began in the Irish peerage: in 1716 she was made Baroness of Dundalk, Lady Marchioness of Duncannon, and Duchess of Munster. As no one protested aside from a few Jacobite pamphleteers, she elevated herself to the English peerage: two years later the King made her Baroness Glastonbury, Lady Faversham, and finally Duchess of Kendal. This insatiable lady now demanded imperial nobility. Vienna could not refuse a request from the King of England, and so in 1722 she was given the title of Princess of Eberstein.

The King, unfaithful in this world, promised he would be faithful to her in the next: if he died before she did, he would come back from the underworld to visit her. So one day when a crow appeared at a window of her residence in Isleworth and refused to be driven away, she was convinced it was George I. She tamed the bird as she had tamed the King, according to Horace Walpole.

Coxe[3] affirmed that the King's other companion, the Baroness, was still most beautiful during the 1720's. This was not the opinion of Horace Walpole, but he was only eight when he saw her. Lady Mary Wortley Montagu and Walpole both saw in this daughter of the wicked Countess Platen another of George's mistresses, who could well be his half-sister. It was said that she bore him a daughter, Sophia Charlotte Margaret, who became Lady Howe. Melville countered this gossip and his arguments seem sound. According to him, the Baroness of Kilmansegg was the daughter of the Elector Ernst August by the Platen woman, who had vainly tried to marry her off to Königsmark. Instead she was married off to the Elector's Master of the Horse, the wealthy Baron von Kilmansegg, and the Elector left her a real fortune. (If all of this is true, it is difficult to understand why she almost had to renounce leaving Hanover to follow George I, because of the alleged refusal of her creditors to let her depart.) Her husband followed her to London, but died in 1717. As a widow she enjoyed a royal pension which seemed to Melville the proof that she was the King's half-sister, given George's avaricious nature. The monarch made no attempt to hide the Baroness of Kilmansegg. She presided over dinners, sitting opposite him, and thus had precedence over the Duchess of Kendal, who never forgave her for this.[4] Not wishing to be outdone by the favorite, the Baroness became Countess Leinster in 1721, and the following year Baroness Brentford and Lady Darlington. Thus she too passed in a two-phase operation from the Irish

---

[3] *Life of Robert Walpole.*
[4] Lady Cowper, *Diary*, 1714–20.

to the English peerage. To believe Lady Mary Wortley Montagu, the Baroness Kilmansegg was a brilliant, well-read woman. The Prince of Wales added that she was distinctly inclined to male company although (according to Lady Cowper) she never failed to brandish a certificate of fidelity signed by her late husband. She died in 1725.[5]

Europe was to be English for half a century, but Marlborough's victories proved very costly. The national debt, inflated by the spending of the last Stuarts, was enormous. On the one hand the young Bank of England was heavily in debt, while on the other hand the new colonial companies were reaping colossal profits. (The East India Company paid a dividend of 4,000 percent.) The South Sea Company offered to take over a good part of the national debt in exchange for its own shares. This proposal by Sir John Blunt, the company's director, attracted statesmen who did not understand much about it. The Commons voted in favor of the scheme, ignoring the recent catastrophe in France that had ended the career of John Law. (Between their Pretenders to the throne and Law, the Scots cost the French a great deal.) The House of Lords and the Bank of England were more obstinate. Nonetheless, the South Sea Company was authorized to acquire most of the national debt, for everyone was convinced that its profits would suffice to reimburse the State and its creditors.

---

[5] The French charge d'affairs in London, Monsieur de Chammorel, wrote when he announced her death: "I have heard that there is a secret intrigue among the Germans at court to bring over a lady from Hanover of honest character to replace the deceased in the good graces of the master, but the Duchess of Kendal . . will certainly find the means to stop this attempt."

The English, being born gamblers not content with lotteries alone, rushed to buy the shares. In Change Alley, the Wall Street of London, the price of the shares shot up from 130 to 1,000. The speculation was so intense that the drama lasted only six months—even less time than it had in France.

Following the example of the South Sea Company, hundreds of small companies sprang up in the city, one more bizarre than the other: a company for salvaging flotsam and jetsam washed up on the coast of Ireland . . . a company to sell human hair . . . a company to manufacture a perpetual motion wheel . . . there was even a company "whose object would be revealed only after it had been floated"; in one morning a thousand subscribers rushed in to put down two guineas each.

Things rapidly took a turn for the worse. When asked about the future of the market, Newton replied that he calculated the movements of celestial bodies, not those of popular folly.

Losses began to make inroads in all social classes. An apothecary, taking the pulse of a patient, exclaimed:

"Ah! It's really dropping terribly . . ."

"Do you mean to say that I'm going to die . . ."

"You are fine. I was thinking of my shares . . ."

To the joy of the Bank of England, the South Sea bubble burst. The shares, priced at £1,000 each, went down £350 a week. At the end of a month they were unsalable. Those who held the shares too long were ruined. A certain Lord Chandos lost £300,000; the Duke of Portland and Lady Mary Wortley Montagu were royally fleeced.

Robert Walpole, who had expressed his disapproval of the venture, and who above all had gotten out in time, was called to head the government. A secret commission of inquiry was named, and the directors of the South Sea Company saw their possessions seized. But the really guilty parties got away. The chief cashier, Robert Knight, was saved by fleeing to the Continent with his account books, which listed the names of the most compromised people.

The royal family had been in the South Sea Company to the hilt.[6] George I had recommended the scheme when he opened Parliament in November. He was urged on by Lady Kendal who, like the rest of the King's German entourage, was paid in shares. There was even talk of the King's abdication in favor of the Prince of Wales. But the latter had lent the distinction of his name to a fancy company involved in copper mining.[7]

The reader will recall the prediction made by the fortuneteller Deborah, which Horace Walpole mentioned, and how George I closely supervised the health of Sophia Dorothea during the thirty-two years of her captivity. If he did not care for her well-being, he found it at least as precious as his own. But how could doctors counter eternal despair? Sophia Dorothea succumbed to brain fever. In her long delirium she cried out her horror at the man to whom her father had bound her. Day by day she grew weaker until, on November 13, 1726, at sixty-one years of age, she breathed her last. Before dying she had written a letter that was entrusted to safe hands.

When he had word of her death from Ahlden, George I was seized with terror. He trembled when he learned of her long and frightening agony, her curses, her threats,

---

[6] J. Carswell, *The South Sea Bubble* (1959).
[7] Anonymous, *Mémoires du règne de Georges 1er*.

and the frightening way in which she had promised to meet him before the tribunal of God.

Nowhere in England was a public announcement made about Sophia Dorothea's death. When he heard that the court of Hanover had gone into mourning, George I became violently angry and immediately countermanded it. He forgave neither the court of Berlin nor his daughter, the Queen of Prussia, for having gone into mourning. The *London Gazette* noted only: "Death of the Dowager Duchess of Hanover."

The Prince of Waldeck, who had brought the news to London, returned to Germany with instructions to have Sophia Dorothea buried in the garden at Ahlden.

In the Palace of St. James, George I continued to tremble. The fears of the superstitious Kendal only fed his own. Every day she told the King that the shade of the dead woman would find no rest until her body had been buried with her family in the church at Celle. The King finally ordered it done, and the transfer was made at night, without a religious service being said. The remains of Sophia Dorothea still lie today in the quiet little city of Celle, which has since then been spared the consequences of men's anger and whose friendly surroundings seem so inappropriate for tragedy. But there is nothing at Celle to recall even her name, although the German nobility habitually had their names inscribed on their tombs so as not to be confused with the common people at the Last Judgment.

The hatreds of the descendants of Atreus[8] are the worst kind; they wore the King down. He could find no rest. Unable to sleep, he went to the theater every evening.

[8] Atreus, King of Mycenae, was the father of Menelaus and Agamemnon. The family was tragically notorious for their numerous murders, parricides, adulteries, and cases of incest. — Trans.

What Madame de Maintenon called "a spirit of dizziness" reigned at the Palace of St. James. Germans in the eighteenth century were haunted by superstitions; England was the land of ghosts, and George I reigned over both countries. He was a man without a conscience and his remorse, buried under his great bulk, stirred only below the surface, unbalancing this ponderous statue of flesh and gold, the soul of "this cold and obstinate man." He was all distrust and silence, and, as the Princess Palatine said, the words had to be dragged out of him. He hovered, irresolute and sullen, like those men condemned to death in absentia whose effigies were hanged at the gates of the palace at Hanover—those paper ghosts that had frightened him when he was a child.

On May 3, 1727, a month after Sophia Dorothea had been laid to rest for the last time, when spring had come, he decided to leave for Hanover.

He was sixty-eight and this was his sixth trip.[9]

The King of England was returning home to Germany. He was going back to where he started, as an eel returns to its native estuary. He was not one of those cosmopolitan people who consider the world their homeland. In London, Venice, Versailles, or Hungary, he had camped, ever the soldier ordered about by fate, never a wanderer or an idler.

His life had been a closed circle. London was an open door onto a world that was to be British for two centuries; a civilization built on the ruins of the Spanish, Portuguese, Dutch (and soon the French) colonial empires. But George had seen nothing, guessed nothing, and loved nothing about this world.

---

[9] The others took place in 1719, 1720, 1723 (twice), 1726.

Neither his altered surroundings nor his unexpected and unsolitited success in life had roused him or made him renounce his foul habits and his egoism. He could certainly equal his British subjects for phlegm.

The only poetic touch in this existence was something he never even suspected, namely, the strange premonition which impelled him to return to Hanover at this time. Narrow-minded as he was, he found himself moved by a curious inspiration, rather like a dream of destiny. He was caught up in an infernal movement, swept by a secret tide away from his adopted country and impelled to return to his native land.

On each occasion he had left his kingdom like a schoolboy on holiday to come back to Hanover where as soon as he arrived "he forgot the accident that took place on August 1, 1714." That is how Lord Peterborough described the day on which George Louis had become king! Like a schoolboy asking to leave the classroom, George I had to ask Parliament's permission to leave England. The Act of Settlement included that stipulation, for everyone feared a royal desertion.

According to Horace Walpole, the King's last and tardy homage to England was to take as his mistress the extremely pretty daughter of a colonel. She was named Maria Garetta Brett, and was very dark and rather Spanish-looking. When the King took up with her, his subjects were at once scandalized and flattered. "Debasing his gallantry," George fell into what the Marquis d' Argenson called in his *Mémoires* "monogamous whoring." Whether out of regret at leaving the pretty Brett or because of a less conscious apprehension, the King for the first time—according to Horace Walpole—took leave of the Prince and Princess of Wales with genuine emotion, saying that he would never see them again.

George I left from Greenwich and arrived in Holland the next day. The squadron that escorted him dropped anchor near Utrecht at the mouth of the Meuse River.

He reached the German frontier on June 19, 1726. During a halt at Dalden at eleven o'clock at night, he ate a large supper, including an entire melon, and ordered the departure for three o'clock in the morning. Leaving Lady Kendal in Dalden, he set out for Osnabrück in his coach. It was scarcely light as the coach rolled along between windmills, making a frightful noise on the cobbles. At the edge of town a stranger stepped forward with a letter in his hand. Petitions were frequently presented to the King in this way, but usually a member of his suite would receive them. This time the stranger asked permission to deliver the letter into the King's own hands.

As soon as it was daylight, George I opened the letter and turned pale. It was from Sophia Dorothea! The messenger had waited for him at the frontier, as patient as death.

In the letter Sophia Dorothea promised to meet George before the tribunal of God one year and one day after the death of his sacrificed wife.

He calculated that he had only six months to live.

His arm trembled convulsively; his tongue shot out of his mouth. He suffered a heart attack in the arms of his chamberlain, Fabricius.

"C'en est fait de moi" ("I'm finished"), he murmured in French.

He was bled at Linden. They tried to make him lie down, but he motioned that the journey must continue at all costs, and he stammered "Nach Osnabrück . . . nach Osnabrück" ("To Osnabrück . . . to Osnabrück").

The coach arrived in Osnabrück at ten in the evening. According to Horace Walpole, Jesse, and Coxe, the King, who was thought to be asleep, was found dead in the coach. Malortie asserted that he died only on arrival at the bishop's palace that had been built by his father and where his brother, the new Prince-Bishop, now lived.

This brings to mind a letter written by the Princess Palatine of March 6, 1718: "I fear that George Louis will come to a bad end."

History
of the Correspondence
Followed by a
Bibliographical Note

The many British and German historians who have studied the period and the people described here are unequally divided between the partisans of Sophia of Celle[1] and supporters of George of Hanover, her husband.

Both parties base their cases on indisputable facts reported by contemporarie or by commentators living shortly thereafter. These sources include the anonymous author of the *Histoire secrette de la Duchesse de Hanover* (1732) (although it is rather novelistic), the *Mémoires de George Ier* (1729), the *Mémoires* of Gourville, the *Correspondance* of Elisabeth-Charlotte d'Orléans, the *Mémoires* of Pollnitz (1740), the account by Toland, *La Cour de Hanovre* by Malortie, the roman clef entitled *Römische Octavia* (1707) by Duke Anthony Ulrich of Wolfenbüttel, and finally, the imprecise but amusing *Reminiscences* by Horace Walpole and the *Letters* of Lady Mary Wortley Montagu.

---

[1] Spelled variously Celle, Zelle, or Zeel, from the Latin *cella*.

Two centuries after the events the historian W. H. Wilkins of Cambridge University emerged as the chief defender of the unfortunate Princess. He has the distinction of having first published the correspondence between the heroine and Königsmark in *The Love of an Uncrowned Queen* (1900). At the head of the opposing camp was Lewis Melville, in whose biography *The First George* (1908), the discredited King George I remains a brave soldier, an honest man, a sort of sage without ambition whose indifference toward his new kingdom assured the rise of British parliamentary government. A. W. Ward, the author of the article on George I in the *Dictionary of National Biography* and of the book entitled *The Electress Sophia,* is rather more in the Melville camp. Both he and Melville are eminently Victorian in spirit.

Melville scathingly accused his adversaries of creating the scenario for a romantic drama. Despite this, and taking into account contemporary observers (particularly the French and British diplomatic representatives in Hanover, for this tragic story fascinated all the courts of Europe), we have adopted psychological analysis as our guide through the labyrinth of contradictory intrigues. In doing so we have endeavored to reconcile an exact with an inexact science: history and love.

The letters begin in July 1690 and end in December 1693. Sophia Dorothea's letters of the first six months of 1694 (the last half year of their relationship) have disappeared, probably seized or destroyed by the Elector of Hanover. The Princess herself doubtless burned the letters she received from Königsmark. Those of Königsmark's letters that have come down to us were probably preserved in Hamburg by Aurora von Königsmark and entrusted by her to her sister, Countess Löwenhaupt. The Löwenhaupts took them to Stockholm when they returned to Sweden.

On the death of Countess Löwenhaupt, her son, Count Charles Emile, inherited the letters. He died without leaving a male heir and entrusted the correspondence to his daughter, who married Baron Hans Ramel of Ofvedskloster.

This daughter, who died in 1810, left the letters to her daughter, Countess G. A. Sparre.

Countess Sparre gave the letters to her daughter, Countess Jacob de la Gardie.

At this time the existence of the letters became public knowledge. Professor W. F. Palmblad of the University of Uppsala, annexed extracts from them to his novel *Aurore de Königsmark* (1847). But his selections contained so many errors that their authenticity was doubted.

When the Count de la Gardie died, the University of Lund inherited the originals of the letters in 1848.

From 1848 to 1850 the letters were copied by J. H. Gadd, assistant librarian at the University of Lund, and the copies were sold to Mrs. Evelyn Everett Green, an Englishwoman who in 1870 sold them to the British Museum.

W. H. Wilkins went to Lund in 1898 to verify the authenticity of the letters. He copied and described them with care. He said that there were two hundred of them written in French but not arranged in chronological order. Wilkins only published two thirds of the correspondence in English translation in his history of Sophia Dorothea.[2]

---

[2] *The Love of an Uncrowned Queen* (1900), Vol. I, p. 173.

Certain letters are in Mlle. de Knesebeck's hand, as dictated to her by Sophia Dorothea.

In 1879 a historian named Dr. A. Kocher judged the letters to be forgeries. This was also the opinion of another scholar, but neither had seen the originals. Doubtless they had worked from the extracts published by Palmblad.

In 1906 the *Dictionary of National Biography* still listed the letters as "disputable."

Wilkins' merit was to compare the details of court life cited in the letters with the same details and dates related in the diplomatic dispatches from the British envoys at Celle and Hanover. He found a perfect correlation.

In July 1754, Queen Louisa Ulrica of Sweden sent her brother Frederick the Great sixty-four letters taken from the Königsmark-Sophia Dorothea correspondence. The correspondence belonged to the family of the Count Löwenhaupt, the husband of Königsmark's sister. It was carefully preserved in their castle before being bequeathed by their descendants to the University of Lund.

It is not known how the Queen came by these letters, which were passed on in disorder and very badly presented. Frederick II made a parcel of these "not very honorable souvenirs," which he sealed and signed with the following words in his own hand: "Love letters from the Duchess of Ahlden to the Count von Königsmark." Frederick kept the parcel at Potsdam until, on his death, it was sent to Secret State Archives. From there, in the nineteenth century, the letters traveled to Merseburg, where the parcel is preserved in the archives of Hanover.

The correspondence as left at Lund comprises 201 pages in the hand of the Princess or that of Eleonore de Knesebeck, and 471 written by Königsmark.

The Berlin archives contain 14 pages by Sophia Dorothea and 54 by Königsmark.

The photocopies of the Hanover archives comprise 1,399 pages, of which 1,282 are from Lund, and 117 from Berlin.

These pages comprise 73 letters from the Princess and 209 from Königsmark.

These letters, found in Berlin, definitely prove the authenticity of the correspondence.

Below are extracts from a paper of October 31, 1966, in which the history of the correspondence and the question of its authenticity are thoroughly explored. The paper is by Mr. Jean-Pierre Mousson-Lestang, lecturer at the University of Lund, and was transmitted to us by Mr. Marc Guyard, Secretary General of the Cultural Section of the French Embassy in Stockholm.

The author would like to avail himself of this opportunity to express his gratitude to Messrs. Marc Guyard and Jean-Pierre Mousson-Lestang.

This correspondence was famous before it came to light, and for two centuries was considered apocryphal before being recognized as authentic. It is the object of a bibliography almost as extensive as the 600 pages that comprise it. Its history is a curious romance at the very heart of a love story.

The exchange of letters began on July 1, 1690, with a note from Königsmark to Sophia Dorothea, and it ended at the end of 1693.

Before leaving for Flanders, Königsmark wrote for a year to his beloved, who only answered him regularly during the duration of the campaign. Interrupted for six months, the correspondence began again during the Princess' stay with her parents at Celle and at Brockhausen. Then, during the second part of the year 1693, Königsmark was again with the army on the Danish frontier. No trace remains of the letters the two exchanged during the first six months of 1694. The letters began with expressions of respectful affection from Königsmark, who wrote like a hero of one of Mlle. de Scudéry's novels, while Sophia Dorothea wrote from the soul in passionate language that already announced the *religieuse Portugaise*. The letters in the Berlin file are in her own hand. They bear the famous inscription in the hand of Frederick the Great: "Love letters from the Duchess of Ahlden to the Count von Königsmark."

Georg Schnath, the most recent commentator on the correspondence, is most critical of the adaptation of the letters made by Boscq de Beaumont and Bernos in 1914. According to him, the authors only wanted to bring out the literary and aesthetic expressions of a great love and to take their place in French epistolary and erotic literature. This caused them to unjustly neglect Königsmark's letters because of his awkward handwriting and wretched French, and to keep only those that were necessary for a knowledge of the facts. The scientific value of the publication was thus diminished—the more so as the selected letters were much rewritten and put into Modern French. Moreover, they were not reproduced from the originals in the archives of Lund, but were simply translated from an English text, which had been prepared by Gadd. Finally, the Berlin letters are absent, for they had not been discovered by the time the book was published.[3]

---

[3] Georg Schnath, *Des Königsmark Briefwechsel*, Hildesheim (1952).

Over the past century this correspondence and the problems of its authenticity have generated an abundant historical or pseudo-historical literature. One of the first of these works was *Aurora Königsmarck und irhe Verwandten* (Orebro and Leipzig), 1847, by the University of Uppsala professor, W. F. Palmblad.

During the second half of the last century, the first doubts of the authenticity of the correspondence appeared in several works by German authors:

W. Havermann: *Geschichte der Lande Braunschweig und Hannover* (1857).

Schaumann: *Sophia Dorothea, Prinzessin von Ahlden und Kurfürstin.*

Adolf Köcher: *Die Prinzessin von Ahlden* (1882).

and a French author:

Horric de Beaucaire: *Une mesalliance dans la maison de Brunswick* (1884).

The following argued for the authenticity of the letters:

the English authors:

W. H. Wilkins: *The Love of an Uncrowned Queen,* London (1900).

A. W. Ward: *The Electress Sophie and the Hanoverian Succession,* London (1909).

the German author:

Robert Geerds: "Die Briefe der Herzogin von Ahlden und des Grafen Philip von Königsmark," *Münchner Allgemeine Zeitung* (1902), No. 77.

Die Mutter der Könige, Munich (1913).

"Die Prinzessin von Ahlden und Graf Ph. Ch. von Köenigsmarck," *Z. Hist. Verin f. Nds* (1915).

the Swedish author:

Birger Mörner: *Maria Aurora Königsmarck en krönika,* Stockholm (1914).

the French author:

G. du Boscq de Beaumont et M. Bernos: *Correspondance de Sophie Dorothée, princesse électoral de Hanovre, avec le comte de Königsmark* (1914).

The most convincing proofs of the authenticity of the letters, which no one in fact seems to have contested since, were offered in 1930 by:

George Schnath: "Der Königsmarck-Briefwechsel — eine Fälschung?", *Niedersächsischen Jahrbuch,* Bd. VII Hildesheim

The same author in 1952 provided a critical edition of this correspondence in which he confirmed his chronological, stylistic, and orthographic conclusions in 1930:

"Der Königsmarck-Briefwechsel," *Quellen und Darstellungen zur Geschicht Niedersaschsens*, Hildesheim (1952).

Then, in 1953, Schnath published:

Der Fall Königsmarck (Eben, Ende und Nachlass des Grafen Ph. Ch. Königsmarck im Licht neuer Funde), Hanover (1953).

According to Schnath, roughly half the correspondence has disappeared, either lost or destroyed. From all points of view Schnath is the best placed to judge the problem of authenticity and one must adopt his conclusions.